Home Grown

THE CASE FOR LOCAL FOOD IN A GLOBAL MARKET

BRIAN HALWEIL

Thomas Prugh, *Editor*

WORLDWATCH PAPER 163

November 2002

FINANCIAL SUPPORT for the Institute is provided by the Richard & Rhoda Goldman Fund, the George Gund Foundation, the William and Flora Hewlett Foundation, The Frances Lear Foundation, the Steve Leuthold Foundation, the Charles Stewart Mott Foundation, the Curtis and Edith Munson Foundation, the John D. and Catherine T. MacArthur Foundation, the NIB Foundation, the Overbrook Foundation, the David and Lucile Packard Foundation, the Surdna Foundation, Inc., the Turner Foundation, Inc., UN Environment Programme, the Wallace Global Fund, the Weeden Foundation, and the Winslow Foundation. The Institute also receives financial support from its Council of Sponsors members—Adam and Rachel Albright, Tom and Cathy Crain, and Robert Wallace and Raisa Scriabine—and from the many other friends of Worldwatch.

Table of Contents

ACKNOWLEDGEMENTS:

I am grateful to the many people who shared their knowledge and criticism for this paper, including Herb Barbolet, Andy Fisher, Jerry Goldstein, Joan Gussow, Ronald Halweil, Mary Hendrickson, Dave Henson, Matt Hora, Ian Hutchcroft, Andy Jones, Jack Kloppenburg, Dick Levins, Katy Mamen, Ilaria Morra, Michael Olson, Rich Pirog, Valeska Populah, Jules Pretty, Mark Ritchie, Wayne Roberts, Peter Rosset, Edward Seidler, Jac Smit, Greg Studen, and Mark Winne. At Worldwatch, many colleagues provided thoughtful feedback on various drafts, including Erik Assadourian, Richard Bell, Chris Bright, and Danielle Nierenberg. Editorial Director Ed Ayres helped shape an earlier article, "Where Have All the Farmers Gone?," which provided the conceptual motivation for this paper. Interns Arunima Dhar and Meghan Crimmins tracked down elusive data and information, while Research Librarian Lori Brown obtained various books and relevant documentation, and also quietly inspired me through her and her husband's own efforts to grow and sell local food. Senior Editor Tom Prugh helped me tighten the language and improve the rigor of the argument. Art Director Lyle Rosbotham advised me on how to make the best use of graphics to convey useful information. Leanne Mitchell and Susan Finkelpearl in Worldwatch's communications office helped me distill the messages I hope this paper will convey.

Research Associate **BRIAN HALWEIL** joined Worldwatch Institute in 1997 as the John Gardner Public Service Fellow from Stanford University. At the Institute, Brian writes on the social and ecological impacts of how we grow food, focusing recently on organic farming, biotechnology, hunger, and rural communities. Brian's work has been featured in the international press and he has testified before the U.S. Senate Committee on Foreign Relations on the role of biotechnology in combating poverty and hunger in the developing world. Brian has traveled extensively in Mexico, Central America, the Caribbean, and East Africa, learning indigenous farming techniques and promoting sustainable food production. Before coming to Worldwatch, Brian worked with California farmers interested in reducing their pesticide use, and set up a two-acre student-run organic farm on the Stanford campus. Brian is the author of two previous Worldwatch Papers, including *Underfed and Overfed: The Global Epidemic of Malnutrition* (March 2000), co-authored with Director of Research Gary Gardner. Brian also co-authored the 1999 book *Beyond Malthus: Nineteen Dimensions of the Population Challenge*.

Summary

People everywhere depend increasingly on food from distant sources. In the last 40 years, the value of international trade in food has tripled, and the tonnage of food shipped between nations has grown fourfold, while population has only doubled. In the United States, food typically travels between 2,500 and 4,000 kilometers from farm to plate, up to 25 percent farther than in 1980. In the United Kingdom, food travels 50 percent farther than it did two decades ago.

The reason is partly demographic: Since more people live in cities, fewer people live near food production centers. Perhaps more importantly, advances in technology that allow longer storage and more distant (and less costly) shipping have encouraged the food system to sprawl. Cheap gasoline and various transportation subsidies also underpin this food traffic, which can require staggering amounts of fuel. A basic diet—some meat, grain, fruits, and vegetables—using imported ingredients can easily gobble four times the energy, and generate four times the greenhouse gas emissions, of an equivalent diet with ingredients from domestic sources.

For those who can afford it, the long-distance food system offers unprecedented and unparalleled choice—any food, anytime, anywhere. But the "global vending machine" often displaces local cuisines, varieties, and agriculture. Products enduring long-term transport and storage depend on preservatives and additives, and encounter endless opportunities for contamination on their long journey from farm to plate. Long-distance food erodes the pleasures of face-to-face inter-

actions around food and the security that comes from knowing what one is eating.

Economists often argue that the long-distance food trade
is efficient, because communities and nations can buy their
food from the lowest-cost provider. But the loss of local food
self-reliance brings a range of unseen costs—to the environment, to the agricultural landscape, and to farm communities.

Instead of selling food to their neighbors, farmers sell into
a long and complex marketing chain of which they are a tiny
part—and are paid accordingly. Evidence from North America,
Asia, and Africa shows that farm communities have not ben-
efited, and have often suffered, as a result of freer trade in agricultural goods. Meanwhile, the supposed efficiencies of the
long-distance food chain leave many people malnourished and
underserved. Farmers producing for export often go hungry as
they sacrifice the use of their land to feed foreign mouths, while
poor urbanites in both the First and Third Worlds find themselves living in neighborhoods unable to attract supermarkets,
green grocers, and healthy food choices.

Fortunately, the long-distance food habit is slowly beginning to weaken under the influence of a young, but surging,
local foods movement. This movement can help restore rural
areas, enrich poor nations, return fresh and wholesome food
to cities, and reconnect suburbanites with the land by reclaiming lawns, abandoned lots, and golf courses to use as local farms,
orchards, and gardens. While a certain amount of food trade
is useful, communities that seek to meet their food needs
locally as much as possible will realize other benefits as well:

• Rebuilding local foodsheds requires rebuilding the local
diversity of crops and food businesses needed to adequately feed
the local population. Farmers producing for the local market
tend to increase the diversity of their plantings—a shift with
advantages for the diets of local people and the ecology of local
landscapes.

• Money spent on local produce at farmers' markets, at
locally owned shops, or on locally produced foods stays in the
community longer, creating jobs, raising incomes, and supporting farmers. Developing nations that emphasize greater

food self-reliance can thereby retain precious foreign exchange and avoid the whims of international markets.

• Local food often costs less than the equivalent food bought on the international market or from a supermarket, because transportation costs are lower and there are fewer middlemen.

The explosive growth in farmers' markets and community supported agriculture (food delivery subscription schemes) is the clearest indication of growing interest in local food. But these sorts of direct marketing arrangements are perhaps the easiest parts of the local food system to rebuild, since they operate under the radar of the conventional food chain—in the niche for fresh, high-quality food connected to a real person—that will never be filled by anonymous supermarkets and multinational food companies.

The food processing and retailing sectors are among the most intensely consolidated links in the food chain. Recapturing these sectors will not be easy. In many communities, the local packing house, slaughterhouse, dairy, cannery, and commercial kitchen are gone. Nonetheless, success on this front could hold tremendous profit-making potential, by allowing larger growers (too big for farmers' markets) and larger food businesses to tap the interest in local foods and by enabling a broader range of consumers to enjoy local foods.

Seizing these opportunities will require farmers to shift from their current role as mass marketers of generic commodities to a more entrepreneurial approach that is responsive to local consumer demands. Farmers will benefit from coming together in marketing cooperatives—allowing them to share marketing, transportation, and distribution capacity—as well as from linking up with other institutions suffering from food-industry consolidation, including restaurants, consumer co–ops, caterers, school cafeterias, and independent grocers.

One relatively new institution that can help facilitate these linkages is the local food policy council. More than a dozen such institutions exist in North America alone, tracking changes in the local food system, lobbying for farmland protection, pointing citizens towards local food options, creating incentives for local food businesses, and generally making policy more responsive to local food needs.

A more diffuse, but potentially more powerful, actor is the food consumer. Consumers may seek out local food because of the superior taste of products harvested at the peak of ripeness and flavor, and because of the high level of control it gives over the food they eat. Well-publicized food safety concerns—such as mad cow disease and genetically modified foods—have stirred consumers everywhere to determine the origins of their food. This depends heavily on shortening the distance between food producers and consumers.

Entering the Foodshed

In a sprawling series of hangar-sized warehouses in the Maryland town of Upper Marlboro, fruit, vegetables, meat, milk, and other foods destined for kitchen tables along the East Coast of the United States sit in mammoth refrigerators. This is the midatlantic regional distribution center for Safeway supermarkets, and the echo off the rafters and the hum of the machinery gives some sense of the immense scale of infrastructure required to ship food around the planet and ensure that it is still palatable when it arrives.

Think of this place as a pit-stop for travel-weary foods from around the world. "Essentially, all produce that is distributed on the East Coast must go through here for quality control, taste and appearance inspection, inventory," explains Matthew Hora of the Capital Area Food Bank, who has studied the history of food distribution in the United States. "So if a lettuce farmer outside Atlanta, Georgia, wants to sell lettuce to a Safeway in Atlanta, it must first be shipped 1,000 kilometers to Upper Marlboro for inspection, then be shipped back down to Georgia," all the while consuming fuel and taking up extra road space—not to mention becoming less fresh.[1]

This arrangement may seem absurd. To a supermarket executive or produce wholesaler, this mammoth distribution center is a state-of-the-art innovation in efficiency. But include the subsidies for gasoline and roads, the effects of smog and global warming, the ecological fallout from the industrial farms that supply the distribution center, and a range of other hidden costs, and the "efficiency" of long-distance food begins to fade away. Because these costs are mostly unaccounted for—not paid directly by the consumer, farmer, or supermarket—the resulting food is artificially cheap.

Food hasn't always been such a globe-trotter. For example, as recently as the 1950s virtually all of the fruits and vegetables consumed in Washington, D.C., were grown on farms in nearby Maryland. Long-distance shipping was impractical and expensive. But a chain of related events over the next few decades changed that. Refrigerated long-haul trucks were developed, and gasoline prices fell. A federally subsidized interstate highway system spread from coast to coast. Advances in food processing made long-term storage possible. California produce growers began advertising aggressively. Before long, the Midatlantic began to depend on food from all over. Statistics from one wholesale market in Maryland show that the average kilogram of produce traveled at least 2,800 kilometers from farm to plate, as much as 25 percent farther today than in 1980.[2]

As local farmland declined in importance and profitability in the Midatlantic, thousands of farmers in Virginia, Pennsylvania, and Maryland went under and farm communities dried up, many of them replaced by subdivisions and asphalt. The landscape declined in diversity as the remaining farms specialized in one or two crops to service distant markets rather than provide a range of foods for locals. The economic landscape also declined in diversity as many food businesses— from local grocers and bakers to local canneries and caterers— were replaced by a handful of national conglomerates.[3]

This system of long-distance food supply has now become the norm in much of the United States and the rest of the world. Apples in Des Moines supermarkets are from China, even though there are apple farmers in Iowa; potatoes in Lima's supermarkets are from the United States, even though Peru boasts more varieties of potato than any other country. Today, our food travels farther than ever before, often thousands of kilometers. The value of international trade in food has tripled since 1961, while the tonnage of food shipped between countries has grown fourfold, during a time when the human population only doubled.[4] (See Figures 1 and 2.)

But, as with many trends that carry serious social and ecological consequences, the long-distance food habit is slowly beginning to weaken, under the influence of a young, but surging, local foods movement in the Midatlantic and elsewhere. Politicians and voters in the counties surrounding Washington, D.C., have supported aggressive measures to protect farmland using tax credits, conservation easements, and greater emphasis on mass transit. Some of this interest is inspired by the desire to preserve the beauty of the countryside, but the campaign to preserve local farmland also rests on the assumption that farmers connected to a community are likely to farm more responsibly. Accokeek Ecosystem Farm, a seven-acre certified organic farm located on the Potomac River in southern Maryland, not only produces food for a weekly food subscription service for almost 90 families (and has started a waiting list because demand is so great), but plays a role in protecting the Chesapeake watershed (farmland holds more water than sprawling subdivisions) and keeping agrochemicals out of the Bay.[5]

Since protecting farmland means little if farmers continue to go out of business, many Midatlantic residents and organizations are bringing back local food markets, which not only help sustain the local farm economy but also build solidarity between farmers and their urban neighbors. This became clear on a recent trip to the bustling FreshFarm Market, staged weekly in a bank parking lot and adjacent side street off Washington's Dupont Circle and hosting about 30 growers from within 250 kilometers of the city. From a distance this farmers' market looks like a human beehive, buzzing with conversation, laughter, music, and talk of food—the social and aesthetic antithesis of the food system symbolized by the Safeway distribution center in Upper Marlboro. (Sociologists esti-

FIGURE 1

Value of World Agricultural Trade, 1961–2000

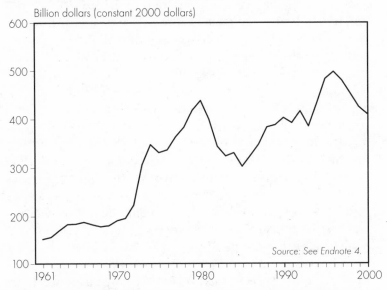

Billion dollars (constant 2000 dollars)

Source: See Endnote 4.

FIGURE 2

Volume of World Agricultural Trade, 1961–2000

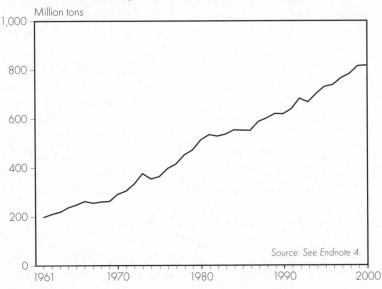

Million tons

Source: See Endnote 4.

mate that people have 10 times as many conversations at farmers' markets than at supermarkets.) Each Sunday, the FreshFarm Market features a different local chef demonstrating how to transform what is currently available at the market into a scrumptious dish—on one August Sunday, how to make a pesto out of garlic and how to can tomato sauce. This is a big draw for market-goers and an easy way to reinforce the possibilities of seasonal cooking. Apart from the tasty fare, "the biggest reason for shopping here," according to market supervisor Bernie Prince, is that in stark contrast to the typical foodchain in which food travels thousands of kilometers and might change hands a dozen times, "a farmers' market allows you to have some firsthand sense of where your food comes from." Such a connection means more to Americans as news reports discuss the possible risks of food irradiation, genetically modified organisms, and bacterial contamination (this last of which recently prompted the second largest meat recall in national history).[6]

Ten other farmers' markets have sprung up around town just in the last year. The farmers' market in Anacostia, the poorest section of Washington, might be the best hope for many residents to get fresh fruits and vegetables—urgently needed in a part of the city crammed with fast food joints but without a supermarket for the last few years. For Anacostia residents, accustomed to conducting food purchases through bulletproof glass, the market also creates a safe, central public place for people to gather and socialize.[7]

Farmers in the region have banded together in a number of marketing cooperatives in order to sell at farmers' markets, deliver weekly boxes of vegetables to private subscribers, and serve commercial kitchens at hotels, restaurants, and cafeterias. The 14-member Tuscarora Organic Growers Cooperative, for instance, supplies several local grocers, natural food stores, and assorted restaurants. "For a chef concerned with taste, there is no substitute for working with food in-season that has been picked the day before," explains Nora Poullion, whose restaurants buy from Tuscarora. Poullion notes that her restaurants could not offer an array of local meats, grains, fruits, vegetables, and nuts without the existence of many local farms, including some local growers who have built greenhouses to extend their growing season.[8]

This interest in local food is almost catching. As more farmers raise a variety of crops for local markets, it can quickly become easier and cheaper for school cafeterias, restaurants, government offices, and households to incorporate local foods into their cuisine. The presence of a farmers' market or community garden often inspires neighboring areas to create their own, and the possibilities for start-up food businesses, including bakeries, butchers, green grocers, canneries, and caterers, multiply with the growing availability of local foods.

This is what it looks like to rebuild a local "foodshed"— that sphere of land, people, and businesses that provides a community or region with its food. So many of these activities and arrangements seem intrinsically valuable: chefs using fresher, tastier, and less processed foods; farmers linking up to offer busy consumers a diversity of products in one location; empty downtown parking lots sprouting farmers' markets on the weekends. But such obviously beneficial developments remain a tiny counterweight to the vast agro-industrial food system, a fact that points to the formidable barriers facing local foods: agribusiness monopolies that can squash competition; cheap fossil fuels that encourage long-distance shipping; a stubborn conception of farmers as producers with no need to connect with eaters; and a range of agricultural policies that discourage local farms, farmers' markets, and food cooperatives in favor of factory farms, megamarkets, and long-distance trade.

The long-distance transport of food has become such a defining characteristic of the modern food system that most people accept it as the only way for us to be well-fed. For those who can afford it, the wonder of eating exotic produce grown halfway around the globe in the depths of a rainforest or on some Asian rangeland emerges as one of the clearest benefits of the long-distance food system. Cheap and fast transportation enable cross-cultural experiences, fusion cuisine, and dietary exploration, especially for those living in large metropolitan centers.

But there is an unavoidable tension between the human enjoyment of variety and the global homogenization of food. The long-distance food system offers unprecedented and unparalleled choice to paying consumers—any food, any time, anywhere. But this astounding choice is laden with contradictions. Ecologist and writer Gary Nabhan wonders "what culinary melodies are being drowned out by the noise of that transnational vending machine," which often runs roughshod over local cuisines, varieties, and agriculture. The choice offered by the global vending machine is often illusory, defined by infinite flavoring, packaging, and marketing reformulations of largely the same raw ingredients. (Consider the hundreds of available breakfast cereals.) The taste of products that are always available, but usually out of season, often leaves something to be desired. And where is the choice when every link in the chain is controlled by a declining number of firms?[9]

Long-distance travel requires more packaging, refrigeration, and fuel, and generates huge amounts of waste and pollution. Products enduring long-distance transport and longterm storage depend on preservatives and additives, and encounter endless opportunities for contamination on their journey from farm to plate. Instead of dealing directly with their neighbors, farmers sell into a long and complex food marketing chain of which they are a tiny part—and are paid accordingly. A whole constellation of relationships within the foodshed—between neighbors, between farmers and local processors, between farmers and consumers—is lost in the process. Farmers producing for export often find themselves hungry as they sacrifice the output of their land to feed foreign mouths, while poor urbanites in both the First and Third Worlds find themselves living in neighborhoods unable to attract most supermarkets and other food shops and thus without healthy food choices. The supposed efficiencies of the long-distance chain leave many malnourished and underserved.

Our food system in many ways reflects what the changing world economic structure means for the environment, our health, and the quality of our lives. The quality, taste, and vitality of our foods are profoundly affected by how and where they are produced, and how they arrive at our tables. Food touches us so deeply that threats to local food traditions have sometimes provoked strong, even violent, responses. José Bové, the French sheep herder who drove his tractor into a McDonald's to fight what he called "culinary imperialism," is one of the better known symbols in a nascent global movement to protect and invigorate local foodsheds. It is a movement to restore rural areas, enrich poor nations, return wholesome foods to cities, and reconnect suburbanities with their land by reclaiming lawns, abandoned lots, and golf courses to use as local farms, orchards, and gardens.

Local food is sprouting through the cracks in the long-distance food system: rising fuel and transportation costs; the near extinction of family farms; loss of farmland to spreading suburbs; concerns about the quality and safety of food and the craving for some closer connection to it. Long-distance food erodes the pleasures of face-to-face interactions around food and the security that comes from knowing what one is eating. (Eating local might be the best defense against hazards introduced intentionally or unintentionally in the food supply, including E.coli bacteria, genetically modified foods, pesticide residues, and biowarfare agents.) On a more sensual level, locally grown food served fresh and in season has a definite taste advantage—one of the reasons this movement has attracted the attention of chefs, food critics, and discriminating consumers around the globe.

The local alternative also offers huge economic opportunities. In every country, money spent on local produce at farmers' markets and locally owned shops stays in the community, cycling through to create jobs, raise incomes, and support farmers. Developing nations that emphasize greater food self-reliance can thereby retain precious foreign exchange and avoid the whims of international markets. There is strong evidence that local food often costs less than the equivalent food bought on the international market or from a supermarket, because transportation costs are lower and there are fewer middlemen.

But despite its many advantages, the local alternative

nevertheless stands against the daunting tide of agribusiness consolidation, the decline of crop diversity, and the loss of food literacy by the average consumer. Change will not come easily. Control of the food system has been largely lost to a dwindling number of food companies. This is what makes the idea of eating locally so radical—the fact that communities around the world all possess the capacity to regain this control by rebuilding local food institutions, such as farmers' markets and small-scale food processing facilities. The explosion of farmers' markets and community-supported agriculture points to the growing numbers of consumers, farmers, and food businesses that have already shifted their role in the food chain, detaching themselves from long-distance cuisine to live within their foodsheds.

The Transcontinental Lettuce

For the better part of human history, and even as recently as several decades ago, most people obtained their food from local sources. Statistics on how far food travels are not available for most nations. Nonetheless, a survey of trends from a number of nations and regions clearly indicates a growing distance between the fields and pastures where most food is grown and the mouths it feeds.

Food trade, for instance, has grown nearly threefold since 1961. Countries shipped $417 billion worth of food and agricultural goods around the globe in 2000. As the value of agricultural trade has increased, so has the volume. Today, some 817 million tons of food are shipped around the planet each year—up fourfold from 200 million tons in 1961. (See Figures 1 and 2, page 11.)[10]

Surveys of food moving within nations tell the same story. (See Figures 3A and B, pages 18 and 19.) Several surveys from different wholesale markets in the United States show that fruits and vegetables are traveling between 2,500 and 4,000 kilometers from farm to market, an increase of roughly 20 percent in the last two decades. Food eaten in the United Kingdom travels 50 percent farther on average than two decades ago. Over the same period, imports of fruits and vegetables arriving there by plane more than tripled, to nearly 120,000 tons a year. Trucks moving food now account for nearly 40 percent of all road freight in the United Kingdom.[11]

Part of the reason we are moving more food around the planet is demographic: there are more people living in cities and fewer living near the centers of food production. Perhaps more importantly, advances in food technology that allow longer storage and more distant (as well as cheaper) shipping helped the food system to sprawl. Even though ice-refrigerated railroad cars allowed perishable food products to be shipped as early as the 1860s, it was major innovations in refrigeration engineering after World War II that gave birth to the frozen food industry. Scientists also developed techniques to control the ripening of fruits, vegetables, and other perishables that further extended shelf-life. Advances in transportation came particularly fast—steamships in the mid-1800s, railroads later in the 19th century, the refrigerated truck in the mid-1900s—and combined with falling oil prices to dramatically reduce the cost of shipping food. It now costs 70 percent less to ship cargo (all items, not just food) by sea, and 50 percent less to ship by air, than it did 20 years ago.[12]

These innovations in food processing and shipping often worked together. For instance, before scientists figured out how to make frozen orange juice concentrate, orange growers could only ship their fruit fresh, and most people in temperate regions enjoyed oranges and orange juice only as a seasonal delicacy. During World War II—partly responding to requests from the U.S. government for an orange juice product that could be shipped to troops overseas—American scientists developed a process for concentrating the orange juice (reducing its bulk and allowing it to be shipped at lower cost), adding a small amount of unconcentrated juice to the mixture (which greatly improved the flavor), vacuum sealing it in cans, and then passing the cans through a freezing tunnel before shipping in refrigerated oceanliners, box cars, and trucks. This

Local Versus Imported Ingredients: Iowa

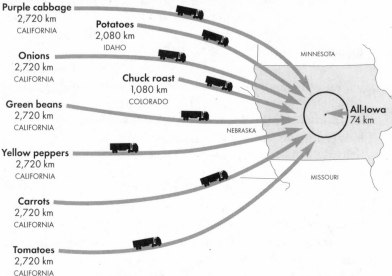

The foods going into an "All-Iowa" meal traveled an average of 74 kilometers to reach their destination, compared with 2,577 kilometers if they had been shipped from the usual distant sources nationwide. Researchers estimated that local and regionally sourced meals entailed 4 to 17 times less petroleum consumption and 5 to 17 times less carbon dioxide emissions than a meal bought from the conventional food chain.

Source: See Endnote 11.

process, still in use, revolutionized the orange growing industry, freeing it from seasonal and geographic constraints, and thereby transformed orange juice into a daily ration for many Americans and Europeans—and turning frozen orange juice into a multibillion-dollar international business.[13]

All this food traffic requires staggering amounts of fuel (and probably wouldn't be feasible without abundant and cheap oil). Among the biggest culprits are those high-value items with relatively low caloric value and high water content, such as cut flowers, fruits, vegetables, and frozen foods. (Nutritionist Joan Gussow of Columbia University describes the

FIGURE 3B

Local Versus Imported Ingredients: England

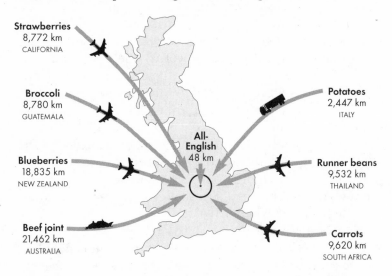

Strawberries
8,772 km
CALIFORNIA

Broccoli
8,780 km
GUATEMALA

Blueberries
18,835 km
NEW ZEALAND

Beef joint
21,462 km
AUSTRALIA

All-English
48 km

Potatoes
2,447 km
ITALY

Runner beans
9,532 km
THAILAND

Carrots
9,620 km
SOUTH AFRICA

A "traditional" Sunday meal in England—beef, potatoes, carrots, broccoli, beans, blueberries, and strawberries—made from imported ingredients generates nearly 650 times the transport-related carbon emissions than the same meal made from locally grown ingredients (almost 38 kilograms of carbon dioxide compared with just 58 grams). All the ingredients are available in England for much of the year except the fruits, which can either be stored or preserved to extend their availability.

Source: See Endnote 11.

process as "burning lots of petroleum to ship cold water around.") The transcontinental head of lettuce, grown in the Salinas Valley of California and shipped nearly 5,000 kilometers to Washington, D.C., requires about 36 times as much fossil fuel energy in transport as it provides in food energy when it arrives. By the time this lettuce gets to the United Kingdom, the ratio of fuel energy consumed to calories provided jumps to 127. "Perishables"—as these goods are known in industry jargon—constitute the fastest growing segment (over 4 percent per year) of the food cargo business and are increasingly shipped by refrigerated plane.[14]

Most international food trade is by boat, and most food trade within nations is by rail or truck, all relatively energy efficient forms of transportation compared with climate-controlled airplane cargo. And products like grains and beans—which pack a great deal of nutrition for a given unit of weight—and coffee, tea, chocolate, and spices can all be shipped dry, without climate control. Nonetheless, Anika Carlsson-Kanyama of Stockholm University has shown that a basic diet—some meat, grain, fruits, and vegetables—with imported ingredients can easily account for four times the energy and four times the greenhouse gas emissions of an equivalent diet with ingredients from domestic sources. In Britain, food transportation is now among the biggest and fastest growing sources of British greenhouse gas emissions— a pattern emerging in much of the world. (The climate changing implications of a long-distance food system are particularly ironic since food production is one of those human endeavors that is most dependent on a stable climate and will be most affected by climatic spasms.)[15]

Much of this shipping seems entirely illogical, as it often involves regions and nations importing food they already have. A recent survey of trade data from the United Kingdom exposed the astonishing reality that the nation imports large amounts of milk, pork, lamb, and other major commodities even as it exports comparable quantities of the same foods, shuttling hundreds of millions of tons of identical food in opposite directions. Analysts explain this "food swap" as an artifact of subsidized transportation, centralized buying by supermarkets and food manufacturers, and trade agreements that set food import quotas even for self-sufficient nations. In the case of milk, British milk purchasers (supermarkets and food manufacturers) prefer to buy a standardized, predictable commodity in large quantities from a few sources—thus forcing British dairy farmers to sell their milk in international markets. These same economic forces also explain why the label on a bottle of Tropicana brand apple juice says it "contains concentrate from Germany, Austria, Italy, Hungary, Argentina, Chile, Turkey, Brazil, China, and the United States." Apart from the questionable cost and pollution, a company buying whatever produce is cheapest on the world market can have no allegiance to place, and the drinker can never really be sure what he or she is drinking. (The above list of countries has a wide range of pesticide standards.) And as ecological economist Herman Daly once remarked about this sort of trade, "Americans import Danish sugar cookies, and Danes import American sugar cookies. Exchanging recipes would surely be more efficient."[16]

Meanwhile, as food ends up farther from the soil in which it was grown, waste loops are broken. Jerry Goldstein, the editor of *Biocycle*, a magazine that tracks trends in dealing with organic waste around the world, notes that the long-distance nature of food systems "creates tremendous food waste disposal pressures at one end, while eliminating an ideal source of plant nutrients and soil-building organic matter for agricultural soils, in favor of polluting chemical fertilizers." (Programs to collect food waste, compost it, and return it to parks, farms, and forest soils have been successfully piloted in supermarkets, restaurants, and residential neighborhoods around the world.) The growth in the distance food travels has also corresponded with an increase in food packaging, as food products are designed for longer journeys and shelf-lives. Food scraps and food packaging now make up a significant share of the waste stream in many cities worldwide. In North American cities, they account for as much as a third of total landfilled waste.[17]

The Wal-Mart Effect

The ability to ship foods long distances created a brutal and fierce competition that pitted farmers and food businesses everywhere against each other. Before long, big national and international conglomerates were muscling in on the traditional markets of local farmers and the neighborhood butchers, bakers, and mom-and-pop grocers. These companies typically offered lower prices and one-stop shopping, had the financial reserves to weather price wars and economic downturns, and often drove the small firms out of business. Among those things lost in this process, which continues today, are the human connections (the butcher who knows your name and favorite cut of meat is replaced by an anonymous employee), some convenience if the supermarket is now farther away than the neighborhood store, and some degree of choice, if you can only buy from one company. Communities also lose some control over their food, since it is harder to influence decision-making in distant corporate offices. Perhaps the biggest loss is the money no longer being recirculated locally, as locally owned businesses, stocking locally made products, are replaced by stores owned by distant corporations and stocked with products from around the globe.

Ken Meter and Jon Rosales, economists at the Cross-roads Resource Center in Minneapolis, describe this process in their recent analysis of the economics of farming in south-eastern Minnesota, a region emblematic of the American Mid-west. Meter and Rosales found that while farmers had sales of $866 million in farm products in 1997, they spent $947 million raising this food, primarily as payments for fertilizer, pesticide, and land made to distant suppliers, creditors, or absentee landowners. (If not for federal subsidies, many of these farmers would not be in business.) Meanwhile, residents of the region spent over $500 million buying food, almost exclusively from producers and companies based outside of the region. In total, Meter and Rosales concluded, the current structure "extract[s] about $800 million from the region's economy each year."[18]

Money, jobs, and food hemorrhaging out of local economies is not a new trend, but it has been a growing one over the last century, as farms become increasingly specialized and more and more services are performed off the farm. As food is shipped long distances, less of the value of that food tends to be retained locally; the shipping, processing, packaging, and retailing of the food assumes greater importance than the food itself. And as more and more of the services once provided by the farm community are out-sourced to other regions or nations, the community retains a declining share of the ultimate profit. In the United States, the share of the consumer's food dollar that trickles back to the farming community has plunged from over 40 cents in 1910 to just above 7 cents in 1997, while the share going to an ever-shrinking number of processing, shipping, brokerage, advertising, and retailing firms has continued to expand.[19]

Think about the business model of Wal-Mart. At a stroke, a new Wal-Mart store can (and does) absorb the business that once flowed into a variety of small, locally owned bakers, grocers, butchers, dairies, farmers' markets, and other outlets. (Wal-Mart, the world's biggest retailer, recently became the world's second largest food retailer.) Any local business is fairly limited in the number of customers it can sell to. But a national or multinational firm can sell to millions of customers in thousands of markets around the world every day. Moreover, consolidation at one link in the chain fuels consolidation at every level of the food business, from the farm to the supermarket retailer. (See Box 1, page 24.) "The relationship between production and marketing is symbiotic," according to Helena Norberg-Hodge of the International Society for Ecology and Culture, a group that studies the impact of globalization on local cultures. "Large-scale, specialized agriculture is best suited to a global and centralized market, and vice versa." It's simply impractical for McDonald's, for example, to source the potatoes for its French fries or the milk for its shakes from thousands of small farms and dairies. (As noted earlier, to keep down transaction costs and to ensure standard products, exporters and other downstream players prefer to buy from a few large producers.)[20]

Economists have long argued that consumers, farmers, and food companies would all benefit from greater trade in foodstuffs, both within nations and between nations, and would argue that this is precisely the reason why this food system has become so dominant. But at the national and international levels, policies have long been biased towards large, specialized farms that are not focused on local markets, and

BOX 1

Concentration in Various Layers of Agribusiness

In 1980, the United Nations Centre on Transnational Corporations published an analysis of the world's 180 most important food and beverage companies, identifying significant levels of market concentration in segments such as dairy, meat, tropical fruits, grain, and tropical beverages. Hope Shand at the ETC Group, based in Canada, recently tried to replicate this study. Shand found that barely a third of the original 180 companies exists today, and that "nearly all of the others have been absorbed into the surviving third." For instance, 65 companies were major competitors in the world pesticide market in 1980. Today, just five companies control 65 percent of the global pesticide market.

Business Sector	Description
Agrochemicals	Five companies control 65 percent of the global pesticide market.
Seeds	The top 10 seed firms control 30 percent of the global seed market; 5 companies control 75 percent of the global vegetable seed market.
Trade	The top five grain trading enterprises control more than 75 percent of the world market for cereals. A handful of transnational companies control about 90 percent of the global trade in coffee, cocoa, and pineapples; about 80 percent of the tea trade; 70 percent of the banana market; and more than 60 percent of the sugar trade.
Meat	One firm controls 60 percent of chicken purchases in Central America. In the United States, four companies control over 80 percent of beef packing, and five companies pack 75 percent of the pork.
Retail	Five retailers control 50 percent or more of all food purchases in France, Germany, and the United Kingdom. Two firms control over 80 percent of Hong Kong's retail market. Between 1994 and 1999, the share of the retail sector in Brazil controlled by the top 10 supermarkets grew from 23 percent to 44 percent. Wal-Mart, the second largest food retailer in the world, recently purchased a major stake in the fifth-largest Japanese food retailer.

Source: See Endnote 20.

against small, diversified farms that are. Subsidies for fossil fuels, roads and other transportation infrastructure, and for commodity production, for instance, all make food shipped round the world in a refrigerated cargo container, wrapped in layers of plastic, and grown on a highly polluting farm look artificially cheap. Proponents of the current system argue that it has suc-ceeded because it is better and more efficient, but this is only true to the extent that many of the costs are not accounted for—from food safety threats to wasteful burning of fossil fuels to a loss of economic life in farm communities.

In many cases, the shift away from local production has not been entirely voluntary. "The more a nation is con-strained—by International Monetary Fund and World Bank loans that require nations to open up markets, by heavily subsidized food imports from the First World which squash local production, by regional and global trade agreements—the less voluntary is that nation's shift towards liberalization," accord-ing to David Seddon, a professor of development studies at the University of Norwich in East Anglia. Many developing nations launched export-oriented agricultural strategies in the 1970s as a response to structural adjustment programs that called for reductions in subsidies for staple food crops in favor of sup-ports for export crops.[21]

This pressure from international institutions continued through the 1990s with trade agreements and organizations that covered food, including the North American Free Trade Agreement (NAFTA), MERCOSUR (a South American trade pact), and the World Trade Organization. Some of this pressure came from politicians, economists, and corporations that strongly believed in open borders as the means to prosperity. Opening domestic agricultural markets, economists typically argue, will help reduce hunger and poverty by stimulating investment in developing world agriculture and generating new export revenue through greater access to First-World con-sumer markets. But in many cases, exports have had completely the opposite effect.[22]

Consider the recent experience of Mexico. As a result of its membership in NAFTA and its ongoing integration into the international food market, Mexico is importing more and more of its corn from the United States and elsewhere. Since NAFTA took effect in 1994, imports of corn to Mexico from the

United States have increased 18-fold and now account for one-quarter of Mexican corn. Corn from the United States is less expensive, largely because its production is heavily subsidized by the U.S. government. But the price tag for Mexico includes a mass exodus of corn farmers from the countryside and the loss of the country's corn diversity.[23]

"Centuries of experience with global trade show that as soon as you open yourself up to global markets," says David Seddon, "the risks are high." On the one hand, international commodity prices can drop and wipe out a nation's export revenues; on the import side, meanwhile, the value of its currency can drop and cause the price of food imports to soar. If Mexico's currency plunges in value or the dollar gets stronger, or there is some other disruption in the global economy, then the cheap American corn could suddenly jump out of Mexicans' reach. This is precisely what happened in 1996, when world grain prices spiked and starving Mexican *campesinos*, who had been driven off their land by the previous two years of low prices, were forced to loot grain cars for food. An analysis of the NAFTA years has shown that while Mexican corn farmers lost money and market share, the price of corn in Mexico skyrocketed. The original center of corn diversity has now become dependent on other nations for a food which pervades its culture, diet, and economy.[24]

In her analysis of the fruit and vegetable export industries in Latin America, *Bittersweet Harvest*, Lori Ann Thrupp describes how local communities can suffer as farmers replace fields growing staple crops for local consumption with baby broccoli, carrots, and other export crops for distant mouths. "In many cases, farmers do not make enough money from the venture to purchase food," Thrupp explains, "so their food security suffers when they are enticed into cash crop production." She notes that in most export-oriented agriculture the main beneficiaries are large companies involved in the processing, packaging, and marketing of these crops, including a growing number of international firms. (Even in nations like the United States and Canada, which are strong enough to shape trade agreements to their advantage, liberalization hasn't helped rural communities. During the NAFTA years, both of these nations have seen commodity prices and farmer incomes plummet, as the companies that trade and process agricultural commodities reaped windfall profits.)[25]

While the idea of complete food self-sufficiency may be impractical for rich and poor nations alike, greater self-sufficiency can buffer nations against the whims of international markets. In fact, rebuilding local food systems might offer the first genuine economic opportunity in farm country in years, a pressing need in view of the huge amounts of money leaking out of rural communities. To the extent that functions associated with food production and distribution are relocated in the community under local ownership, more money will circulate in the local community to generate more jobs and income. This is particularly true if crops are not only grown locally, but also processed locally or served in local restaurants. A study by the New Economics Foundation in London found that every £10 spent at a local food business is worth £25 for the local area, compared with just £14 when the same amount is spent in a supermarket—that is, a pound (or dollar, peso, or rupee) spent locally generates nearly twice as much income for the local economy.[26]

This sort of multiplier is perhaps most important in the developing world, where the vast majority of people are still employed in agriculture. In West Africa, for example, each $1 of new farm income yields an income increase in the local economy ranging from $1.96 in Niger to $2.88 in Burkina Faso—increases that do not come when people spend money on imported foods. And the growing prosperity of millions of small farms in Japan, South Korea, and Taiwan following World War II is widely cited as the major stimulus of the dramatic economic boom those countries enjoyed. These "Asian miracles" provide the clearest evidence that alternatives to export-led growth work and have worked before, according to Peter Rosset, director of the Institute for Food and Development Policy. "For this sort of development to work as it did in East Asia," says Rosset, "the money spent on food must recirculate within the local economy, rather than leak out by depending on foreign food sources." [27]

This is not to argue that every locale should produce all of its food. A certain amount of food trade is natural and beneficial. (Essayist and farmer Wendell Berry has suggested that communities should not be exporting food before local needs are met and should not be importing foods that can be readily produced at home.) Whether North Americans and Europeans continue to depend on imported oranges is less of a concern than whether communities are developing their capacity to meet as many of their basic food needs as possible. To the extent that they are, thousands or millions of local businesses will capture much of the planet's food trade instead of a handful of multinationals. [28]

Making Food Deserts Bloom

The foundation of a local food system is crop diversity. A local population cannot subsist on one or two crops, which is the norm in the midwestern United States or any of the other industrial farming regions of the world. Nor can a local population subsist *economically* on one or two crops. "Crop diversity not only makes a diverse diet possible," says Katy Mamen of the International Society for Ecology and Culture (ISEC), "but it also guarantees the existence of local farmers and a range of food related businesses." Mamen has worked in Ladakh, a small mountainous region in the Indian state of Jammu-Kashmir, which produced nearly all of its own food for generations. But money that Ladakhis used to spend buying vegetables grown locally (or barley milled locally or butter churned locally) now fills the coffers of Coca-Cola, Nestle, and other food companies. "Ladakhis have begun to realize that traditional foods and farming skills are incredibly precious," says Mamen, "and that meeting as many of their basic needs as possible close to home offers a certain freedom from the very unstable flux in the value of their currency." To reawaken interest in the local food culture, ISEC helped start the Women's

Alliance of Ladakh, a group that now has 4,000 members, about one-fifth of the adult population. This group has become a vigorous steward of traditional agriculture, initiating a seed saving program to preserve local crop varieties as well as a market for selling and bartering only local crops, including local varieties of mustard, peas, beans, and barley. The crops must be grown locally by women farmers—a sort of procurement standard that keeps money in the local economy.[29]

Alejandro Argumedo of the Association for Nature Conservation and Sustainable Development (ANDES), a group based in Cuzco, Peru, also knows that efforts to preserve traditional crop varieties are essential for shoring up the local economy. Argumedo explains that polyculture (complex plantings of multiple crops and multiple varieties) requires a highly sophisticated and intimate knowledge of the land—something small-scale, full-time farmers can more readily provide than can the proprietors of large, highly mechanized farms. In the case of the Peruvian Andes, the crop mix often includes dozens of potato varieties, numerous other root crops, and assorted greens, beans, and herbs, all in the same field. ANDES has helped communities set up "Potato Parks," areas of farmland in which networks of farmers are cataloguing the potato varieties (sometimes as many as 40 per farm) as "pre-patented" under international law. Since Peru is the center of global potato diversity—the stock of seed that potato farmers and breeders around the world depend on for resilience against major pest outbreaks or climatic shifts—preserving this local food economy is also of significant interest to the rest of the planet.[30]

There is a strong economic argument to be made for preserving this local crop diversity, since it helps to reduce dependence on expensive agrochemicals and other inputs. Studies have shown that diverse organic and ecological farms, which rely less on purchased inputs and more on taking advantage of the ecological processes in the field, cost less to maintain and make more efficient use of land, nutrients, energy, and other inputs, than do chemical-intensive monocultures.[31]

But there is a strong ecological argument for crop diversity as well. When farmers produce for local (rather than export) markets, their customer base diversifies considerably. The odds of success are consequently enhanced by offering a wider variety of products and so they are encouraged to plant a wider range of crops. Tim and Jan Deane, who run the 13-hectare Northwood Farms in the Teign Valley in Devon, England, greatly diversified their crop mix after shifting to serving the local market through a community supported agriculture (CSA) scheme. When they sold to the wholesale market, the Deanes grew 15 to 18 crops per season, but their mix expanded to between 50 and 60 per season once they refocused on the local market. Their operation also began to turn a profit for the first time since they set up the farm in 1984 (and their vegetables traveled shorter distances to the point of sale.) In this way, local food systems can help counter the overwhelming and ecologically destructive global trend toward monoculture.

The relationship between local crop diversity and the degree of local self-sufficiency holds even for a single type of food. Consider the example of apples in Britain. As recently as 1965, Britain was largely self-sufficient in dessert apples (apples for direct consumption, not canning or baking). This self-reliance depended in part on the production of a wide diversity of apples—there are over 2,000 varieties in the National Collection of the U.K.—that ripened and were harvested throughout the year. Most varieties were harvested in late summer and fall, but early varieties like Discovery and Beauty of Bath ripened in April and May, while late varieties like Cox's Orange Pippen and Greensleeves could be harvested well into the winter. (See Figure 4.) In the last 30 years, as less expensive apples began streaming in from abroad and as supermarkets and apple processors required higher degrees of standardization, British farmers replaced 60 percent of their apple orchards with other crops. British orchards are now dominated by two or three "commercially desirable" varieties with a relatively narrow harvest season, crippling the potential to regain self-sufficiency. Today, only 25 percent of the apples eaten in Britain are home-grown.[33]

One of the strongest implications of the global food

FIGURE 4

Seasonal Availability of a Selection of British Apples

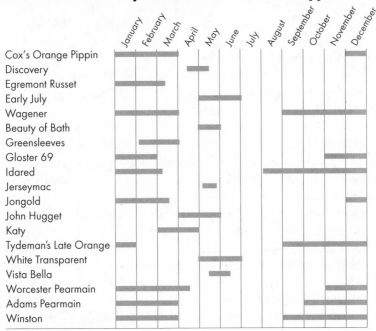

Notes:
1. Early varieties such as Discovery, Early July, and Beauty of Bath cannot be stored for long periods.
2. All other varieties can be stored until late winter and spring of the following year in a traditional fruit store.

Source: See Endnote 33.

chain is that the ability of regions to produce their own food year-round is obsolete. But in those poor communities that are not attractive to distant food companies, the best hope for good nutrition will continue to be local food. As rural areas begin serving distant markets, they produce less and less food for local consumption and must import foodstuffs that could be locally grown, given the right incentives. Fewer home gardens, fewer greenhouses, fewer root cellars, and fewer farmers' markets mean fewer places to sell and buy local produce. Consolidation throughout the food chain has tended to focus on the most lucrative markets, leaving people in remote rural areas with limited food options, such as convenience stores with few nutritious selections and high prices. Doug O'Brien, director of public policy for America's Second Harvest, the nation's largest food relief organization, describes people in the midwestern United States "going to a food bank for a box of cornflakes to feed their children in a community where thousands of acres are devoted to growing the corn for the cornflakes, or even more ironically, for 'feeding the world.'" [34]

Rural sociologists now argue that the term "food deserts," originally coined to describe inner-city urban areas with no green grocers or fresh-food options, is a fitting description of many rural areas. In these areas, there is a strong nutritional imperative to promote local crop diversity. The higher degree of self-reliance afforded by more diversified farms can be an important way of protecting health and nutrition, by ensuring that diets are more diverse, less processed, and richer in fresh fruits and vegetables. Historically, local-source diets have generally been healthy for the people living in the area (except when there was not enough food at all). In fact, nutritionists argue that much of the rise of obesity and obesity-related illnesses around the world can be attributed to the spread of a distinctly non-local diet, that is, the fast-food diet that originated in the United States and is defined by large amounts of meat, fried foods, sugar, and highly processed fare. [35]

The nutritional fallout that comes from the loss of local food diversity has landed heavily on indigenous populations. Treated by governments as second-class citizens, relocated to the poorest lands, and inundated with poor quality surplus food, native people around the world typically suffer from high levels of diet-related illness. The Oodham Indians of the American Southwest, for instance, suffer from one of the highest recorded rates of adult-onset diabetes in the world. But they have found that many of the native, locally available foods that their ancestors enjoyed—like mesquite flour, prickly pear fruit and pads, tepary beans, and cholla buds—are high in fiber and low in cholesterol and saturated fat, and generally help reduce the incidence of diabetes. In addition to the nutritional ben-

efits, recent efforts to revive cultivation of these plants have
have helped to reinvigorate the cultural traditions—harvest cer-
emonies, use as religious offerings, medicinal applications—
tied to the foods. Since 1997, demand for the traditional foods
in the Oodham communities has grown five-fold.[36]

The potential to meet local need from local production
will vary from place to place, particularly where a deficiency
of good soil, appropriate climate, or enough land and fresh
water will prevent major increases in self-sufficiency. But a comparison of local consumption and production patterns can often
point to significant untapped opportunities. Nutritionist Jen-
nifer Wilkins and colleagues at Cornell University studied the
food production and consumption patterns in New York state,
and found that farmers were producing many times more of
some crops (sweet corn, beets, and pumpkins) than could be
consumed locally, but only a fraction of local demand of others (broccoli, carrots, and kale). In the former case, farmers were
forced to sell the surplus into distant wholesale markets. In the
latter, the farmers were missing opportunities to tap into lucrative local markets. "Many of the crops that New York farmers
were underproducing relative to New York demand," Wilkins
notes, "were those same nutritious foods—green leafy vegetables—that are most lacking in New Yorkers' diets."[37]

The notion of local food takes on a very different mean-
ing on a planet where roughly half of the population lives in
cities, a share projected to grow in coming decades. As more
people reside farther from where their food is produced, food
will have to be moved accordingly. Cities may never be able
to satisfy all of their food needs from nearby farmland. But the
tremendous infrastructure, energy, and other costs of shuttling
food into densely populated areas argues for cities to try to
secure as much of their food as possible from farmland within
and near urban areas.[38]

Jac Smit of the Urban Agriculture Network feels that taking advantage of land in and around cities is essential and the
benefits of doing so obvious. Beyond providing urbanites with
a source of fresh food, shifting farming to the cities can spur
food businesses and help urban areas cope with a range of press-

ing ecological, social, and nutritional challenges, from sprawl
to malnutrition to swelling landfills. "In contrast to pure open
space or parks, forms of greenspace which taxpayers generally
have to finance," Smit notes, "urban agriculture can be a
functioning business that pays for itself." In a survey conducted
for the United Nations, Smit estimated that cities already produce about one-third of the food consumed by their residents
on average, using about one-third of their land. (See Box 2,
pages 36 and 37.)[39]

Some nations have shown that there is even more potential. Cuba now depends heavily on urban food production; an
estimated 90 percent of the fresh produce consumed in Havana
is grown in and around the city. This shift to urban agriculture
was largely prompted by the U.S. embargo and then the Soviet
collapse, which left Cuba without agrochemicals, farm machinery, food imports, or petroleum, hobbling Cuba's capacity to
produce food and to ship food from the country to the city.
Confronted with massive shortages of fruit, vegetables, and
other foodstuffs in Cuban cities, government officials set up
a loose network of local extension offices that help Cubans
obtain vacant land, seeds, water, and gardening assistance.
Egidio Paez of the Cuban Association of Agricultural and
Forestry Technicians notes that "the growth and spread of
cities invariably creates many empty spaces... which often
become trash-dumps that are sources of mosquitoes, rats, and
other disease vectors." Cuba's urban farmers raise food without pesticides or chemical fertilizers, and the close proximity
to lots of people makes urban agriculture particularly suited to
such organic food production.[40]

Unfortunately, city politicians, businesses, and planners
continue to regard food as a rural issue that does not demand
the same attention as housing, crime, or transportation, according to Kameshwari Pothukuchi of the Department of Geogra-
phy and Urban Planning at Wayne State University in Detroit,
Michigan. This neglect, and the fact that many urbanites take
the food system for granted, have been reinforced by the
nature of the long-distance food system itself, which ensures
that "even when suburbs and exurbs swept through previously

rural terrain, the loss of local farmland that historically served cities went unnoticed in local grocery stores."[41]

But as Cuba's experience shows, local food production might be the best option for feeding those urbanites who have been neglected by the long-distance food chain. In both the industrial and the developing worlds, poorer urban households typically spend a greater share of their income on food than wealthier urbanites, partly because poor households cannot afford to buy food in bulk and partly because inner-city slums have a shortage of food shops. In the First World, supermarkets have departed the inner cities to milk the more lucrative suburban markets, after pushing many of the independent mom-and-pop grocers out of business and leaving whole city neighborhoods with only fast-food joints and convenience stores.[42]

Wayne Roberts of the Toronto Food Policy Council feels that local agriculture might have an even wider impact on urban and suburban welfare: first, by supplying urbanites with more fresh fruits and vegetables, and second, by affording them the exercise involved in raising food. Roberts notes that obesity is epidemic in Canada, as in most wealthy nations and even in many Third World cities, and that the presence of food production in cities can radically change people's attitude towards food: "Instead of pop and candy vending machines plastering the cityscape, people see fresh fruits and vegetables."[43]

Farmers as Entrepreneurs

Groups like the Women's Alliance of Ladakh and ANDES know that growing food is only the first step in preserving local crops and local farming. The farmers need a market. This is why ANDES has been reviving the east-to-west food trading corridor started by the Incas thousands of years ago (which stretches from the Andean highlands in the west to the Amazonian lowlands in the east) and plans to open a restaurant in Cuzco that will feature local foods. Farmers and local com-

BOX 2

Farming the Cities

People have been growing food in cities for thousands of years. (The hanging gardens in Babylon, for instance, are an example of urban agriculture, while residents of the ancient desert cities of Iran, Syria, and Iraq produced vegetables in home gardens.) This is partly because cities have traditionally sprung up on the best farmland—the same flat land that is good for farming is also easiest for building—and partly because the masses of people in cities creates a great market for fresh fruits and vegetables.

Urban agriculture does, however, pose certain problems, such as theft, poor sun-exposure because of surrounding buildings, and pollution. The risk of contaminants in the soil, like heavy metals or dioxins, as a result of car exhaust or urban industry means that most urban farmers and gardeners need to test their soil before planting. (Rural soils, exposed to decades of agrochemical use as well as possible industrial toxins, are not immune to this problem either.)

These concerns and other characteristics of the urban landscape force city farmers to be particularly creative and resourceful. Gardeners in Vancouver, British Columbia, and Bogotá, Colombia, are taking advantage of the abundant and well-lit surface area on rooftops by raising fruits, vegetables, salad greens, and sprouts there. Farmers and fishers on the eastern coast of Calcutta, India, raise fish and vegetables in marshes fed by the city's nutrient-rich sewage. In Rosario, Argentina, slum dwellers sort the organic matter out of the city's garbage and compost it for use in their own gardens or to sell as a fertilizer.

Worldwide, the United Nations Development Programme estimates that 800 million people are engaged in urban agriculture, the majority in Asian cities. Of these, 200 million are producing primarily for the market and the rest are raising food for their own families.

Similar evidence of extensive urban agriculture can be seen elsewhere:
Africa—In Dar-Es-Salaam, Tanzania, Africa's fastest growing city, urban agriculture is the second-largest source of employment. In 1999, urban farms produced 90 percent of the leafy greens consumed in the city. Bamako, Mali's capital city, is self-sufficient in vegetable production, and urbanites raise much of the city's milk, butter, and meat. Studies from several African cities have shown that families engaged in urban agriculture eat better, as measured by caloric and protein intake or children's growth rates.
Asia—In Hanoi, it is estimated that 80 percent of fresh vegetables, 50 percent of pork, poultry, and freshwater fish, and 40 percent of eggs originate in urban and periurban areas. In Shanghai, 60 percent of the vegetables, more than half of the pork and poultry, and more than 90 percent of milk and eggs originate in the city. In Bangkok, the vast majority of leafy vegetables, such as Chinese mustard, spinach, or lettuce, are grown within the city.
Latin America—In the Brazilian Amazon, one in three households in the city of Belém grow food, medicinal plants, or domestic animals. In Cuba in 1999, the

Box 2 *(continued)*

last year for which there are good data, urban farmers produced an average of 215 grams of fruits and vegetables per day per person, and, in many cities (including Havana, Cienfuegos, and Sancti Spiritus) the average well exceeded the 300-gram-per-day target set by Cuban health ministers. Much of this production came from the 104,087 small urban and suburban gardens in the form of patios, container plants, and "popular gardens" in small spaces between houses and streets.

Europe—More than half of the nearly 5 million residents of St. Petersburg grow some food in back yards and basements, on rooftops, in vacant spaces near houses, or in dachas on the city edges. In the Portuguese capital of Lisbon, where almost one-third of the country lives, farms that grow vegetables, flowers, and wine-quality grapes are common along roadsides or in the spaces left by urban sprawl. Almost 10 percent of Greater London's area is farmland, controlled by around 30,000 allotment gardeners, including 1,000 beekeepers.

North America—In the United States, 79 percent of total fruit production, 69 percent of vegetables, and 52 percent of dairy products are grown in metropolitan counties or fast-growing adjacent counties. The number of community gardens in Toronto more than doubled from between 1991 and 2001, from 50 to 122, and a Toronto nonprofit has made a successful business of growing sprouts and other specialty vegetables on the roof of a warehouse.

Source: See Endnote 39.

munities hoping to take back some of the food economy from distant multinationals will need to provide more of the processing, packaging, and marketing services that have moved off the farm and out of sight. Communities with these varied capacities can replace the vertical integration that now takes place at the corporate level, in which one multinational controls the means of crop production, processing, distribution, and retailing.[44]

This entrepreneurial approach to farming is, unfortunately, unknown to most farmers, and has long been neglected in agricultural training and policy. Jules Pretty of the University of Essex notes that in both the post-World War II policies of the industrial world and the Green Revolution policies of the Third World, "the major message to farmers was to just get on with producing the stuff [food] and leave the other links in the chain to someone else." (Not surprisingly, this attitude coincided with the advent of subsidies for commodity production and the arrival of the first supermarkets in North America and Europe.) In developing nations, simply producing enough raw food for growing populations seemed to be the biggest challenge and became the top priority. "What little emphasis there is on marketing tends to focus on mass marketing of generic agricultural commodities," says Pretty. A British government commission that identified substantial business opportunities in local foods also noted that, for nearly half of farmers, lack of technical knowledge—about growing new crops or a more complex crop mix, food processing, and business and marketing—was one of the main barriers to developing a local food business. This lack of an entrepreneurial emphasis seems to be widespread in the developing world as well. Pretty surveyed over 200 agricultural development projects from Asia, Africa, and Latin America, and found just 12 to 15 percent to have any sort of marketing or processing component.[45]

Farmers' cooperatives, which farmers form to increase their collective power, have also reinforced this neglect of marketing. The traditional cooperative, with its focus on a single commodity, has pigeon-holed the farmer into producing the lowest value input in the food chain. Survival in the modern food chain demands a much different sort of farmers' group and a move from the single-commodity focus of the past to a strategy that is more nimble and more attentive to local consumer demands.

Farmers' markets are perhaps the most obvious example of farmers taking back some of the profits captured by agribusiness, and the most obvious outlet for people wanting to support local farms. The available data show that interest in this institution is soaring. The number of farmers' markets in the United States has grown from nearly 300 in the mid-1970s to 1,755 in 1994 and more than 3,100 today. Approximately 3 million people visit these markets each week and spend over $1 billion each year. Just a few years after the first farmers' market opened in Bath in late 1997, the United Kingdom now boasts over 300, with an estimated $100 million in annual sales. (These statistics refer to the recent movement in which farmers are behind the stalls, not the long history of produce markets run by non-growers dating back to the beginning of history in most countries around the world.)[46]

Farmers' markets not only help the farmer retain a greater share of what is spent on the food—growers retain more of every dollar they take in, compared with selling their goods to the wholesale market—but the absence of middlemen may also mean lower prices for consumers. Case studies from places as diverse as the United States, the United Kingdom, and Costa Rica show that a given basket of produce purchased at a farmers' market is often cheaper than the same produce purchased at a nearby supermarket. In a food system defined by standardization, mass distribution, and economies of scale, farmers' markets also seem to be ideally suited for small or beginning farmers, offering them an opportunity to market relatively small volumes of produce and to experiment with new crops and products.[47]

Another popular form of direct marketing, already mentioned, is subscription farming, or community supported agriculture arrangements, a name that implies some of the social and economic bonds associated with the arrangement. Members of a subscription scheme generally pay the farmer for a yearly share of the farm's output before the start of the growing season and then receive regular deliveries of fruits and vegetables as they become available. (Members might also volunteer, or be required, to help in farm chores or marketing activities.) Many CSA schemes donate shares to needy families, soup kitchens, halfway houses, and food banks, or offer sliding scale subscriptions to ensure that their clienteles are not just the wealthy. Again, where data are available, they show that interest in this institution is growing rapidly. The number of CSA operations in the United States has grown from one in 1985 to over 1,000 today. In the United Kingdom, there are now over 200 certified organic vegetable box delivery schemes alone.[48]

Beyond the standard economic benefits of dealing directly with the customer, the up-front payment bolsters the farmers' cash flow. Because subscribers expect to receive whatever crops are thriving, the farmer has a guaranteed outlet for in-season produce and unexpectedly big yields. Like the farmers' market shopper, the subscriber gets produce that doesn't have to travel far or have a long shelf-life, and therefore is likely fresher, tastier, harvested at the peak of ripeness, and yet not fumigated, refrigerated, or packaged. Subscription schemes and farmers' markets can also both play a role in raising awareness of food-related issues among consumers, using newsletters or simple conversation to share recipes, nutrition advice, or information on political issues that affect farming.[49]

The success of these direct marketing efforts points to the serious constituency for rebuilding local foodsheds. This success is, to some extent, a testament to the high quality of the produce and the social interactions they offer. But these direct marketing schemes might also be the easiest part of rebuilding a local foodshed, in the sense that farmers' markets, CSA arrangements, and other direct marketing schemes operate under the radar of the conventional food chain, in the niche for fresh, high-quality food connected to a real person that will never be filled by anonymous supermarkets and multinational food companies.

As farmers get into the business of processing and adopt more sophisticated marketing schemes, finding space in a market dominated by giants will be a major challenge. Some of the most intense consolidation in the food chain has occurred at the end farthest from the farmer—in processing, distribution, and retailing—and these markets are now closely guarded. "In trying to get beyond the exchange of raw fruits and vegetables," says Andy Fischer, director of the U.S.-based Community Food Security Coalition, "it's not easy to find the local packing house or slaughterhouse or cannery. In most communities, the dairy is gone, the cheesemaker is gone, even the bakery is gone, because of intense consolidation and mergers in agribusiness."[50]

Today's food processing and retailing units tend to be very large and centrally located, making them inconvenient to smaller, local initiatives. There needs to be "something between Sysco and CSAs," explains Jack Kloppenburg, a sociologist at the University of Wisconsin, referring to the largest institutional food supplier in North America ($22 billion in annual sales). This daunting void "between Sysco and CSAs" may hold the greatest money-making opportunity for communities, allowing larger farms and food companies to tap into the interest in local foods and making it possible for a broader range of consumers to buy local foods.[51]

Taking Back the Market

Many of these opportunities will be too ambitious and complex for any one farmer to tackle, and so launching these mid-level food start–ups will often depend on farmers pooling their resources in ways that have not always been typical for the farm community—a community defined by independent-minded folks.

Consider the work of the Association for Better Land Husbandry (ABLH) in Kenya. This group helped to set up and coordinate 16 marketing cooperatives so that local growers can capture the marketing and distribution advantages that come with scale. "Instead of each of several thousand farmers buying their own delivery truck and setting up their own marketing offices," says Jane Tum, an ABLH extensionist, "the cooperative can pool its resources for a much larger delivery truck and marketing staff." Co–op produce is now selling in both local and national markets under the "Farmer's Own" brand name. The co–op also markets energy bars, cooking sauces, and other food items made from locally produced crops as a way to earn farmers a higher price for their harvest than it gets in the raw form. Another group in Kenya, the International Center for Insect Physiology and Ecology (ICIPE), has helped farmers shift over to the cultivation of various aromatic and medicinal herbs, which are made in local processing shops into a product called NaturRub (a remedy for chest colds named after the better-known Vicks VapoRub, which NaturRub is now competing against in Kenyan supermarkets).[52]

These projects are in stark contrast to efforts by the

Kenyan government to promote the horticultural export market. In that scheme, the ultimate customers for flowers and vegetables are European consumers thousands of kilometers away and most of the profits leave Kenya. But the organizers of the ABLH and ICIPE cooperatives have enough market savvy to know that "NaturRub and Mchuzi Mix [a cooking sauce] will not be the farmer's ultimate economic salvation," says Jim Cheatle, the director of ABLH. "The trick is to teach farmers how to innovate, to develop a new product, and to expand into local markets," all skills that Cheatle knows are not typically taught to farmers.[53]

This lack of information and expertise seems to be a particular problem in the case of small-scale food processing. "Farmers are rarely trained in basic processing of agricultural products," according to Sue Azam-Ali, coordinator of agro-processing programs at the International Technology Development Group (ITDG), "even though such processing can be a major source of jobs and additional income." ITDG links up with local organizations to provide training and support to would-be food processors and entrepreneurs. The emphasis is on businesses that are flexible, require little capital investment, and can be run in the home without the need for sophisticated or expensive equipment. Among the projects are cereal milling in Peru, snack food production in Bangladesh, and fruit and vegetable drying in the Sudan.[54]

One of the more successful projects involved making peanut butter in Zimbabwe. After a factory closing that left their husbands out of work, four women living in Chitungwiza, a satellite town of Harare, decided to go into the peanut butter business. They realized that the peanut butter they and their neighbors were regularly buying was made by foreign-owned companies, using imported nuts. They thought that if they could buy peanuts from local farmers, they could produce the butter locally and more cheaply, saving households money and supporting local growers. With the help of ITDG, the women formed Fadzavanhu Enterprises, developed a business plan, and secured a small loan to buy an electric mill. "The project has reached a high level of self-sufficiency, is turning a serious profit, and has been completely handed over to local management," Azam-Ali notes with pride. Fadzavanhu is now investing in a second mill, and locals can rent time on these mills to grind their own nuts. Local testimonials confirm the high quality of the Fadzavanhu product, which sells in local stores and supermarkets for 15 percent less than mainstream brands. (Women, who traditionally possess cooking and other food-processing skills, are particularly well positioned to make money from agroprocessing ventures.)[55]

"For the developing world, in particular, local processing capacity not only offers an opportunity to make extra money," according to ITDG's Azam-Ali, "but also helps to maintain the supply of food throughout the year." Relatively simple drying, canning, pickling, and other processing techniques allow a family to "put up" food for a later date—a form of insurance against crop loss or the seasonal dip in food availability between harvests, and a potential solution to the large quantities of food currently wasted around the world due to poor transportation and storage.[56]

Even after farmers and food businesses have made the decision to process and sell foods locally, breaking into the local market may pose a daunting challenge. (Many ITDG projects, for example, are now experimenting with shops attached to their processing centers, a response to feedback from their entrepreneurs who lack markets for their goods.) In many countries, food retailing is dominated by a declining number of multinational supermarket chains, which wield awesome power over which food products are, and are not, seen by shoppers. Major supermarket chains charge food manufacturers tens of thousands of dollars in "slotting fees" for prize space on the supermarket shelves—fees that small groups of farmers or small-scale food businesses cannot afford. In the industrial world, at least, most people do the vast majority of their food shopping at supermarkets, so any local efforts to recapture this market will depend partly on replicating the convenience and product offerings that people have come to expect when they shop for food.[57]

One promising innovation spreading across Europe is

the "farm shop," in which a group of farmers who produce a variety of products join together to acquire and manage a food store that sells their products exclusively. (The store might sell some imported products during the local off-season.) The model seems to make economic sense, succeeding in several different nations and settings without government support. The growers guarantee themselves a regular market for larger volumes of food than can be sold at a weekly farmers' market, while time-conscious consumers can still do most of their shopping at one store that's open six or seven days a week. Tagwerk, for instance, is a Bavarian eco-regional cooperative of farmers, bakers, and butchers that runs seven Tagwerk shops, two "biomobiles" (mobile market stalls), five bakeries, and three butchers' shops. The 180-member cooperative is diverse enough that it can stock Tagwerk's stores with nearly all of the basic goods a typical consumer would need, and the scale of business is large enough that Tagwerk can employ over 40 people, mostly part-time, in addition to the farmers.[58]

Mary Hendrickson of the University of Missouri Food Circles Networking Project suggests that "to expand their marketing and distribution opportunities, farmers can form alliances with other players getting nuzzled out in the ongoing process of consolidation," including independent supermarkets, schools and universities, consumer food cooperatives, chefs and restaurateurs, and hotel owners. This sort of alliance can help arrest the positive feedback loop that makes it harder and harder for independent players to survive.[59]

Following are a few examples of institutions that link local food to local food business:

Food Processing

• Founded in 1946 by a few dozen dairy farmers in India and now selling a full line of dairy products under the Amul brand, the Gujarat Cooperative Milk Marketing Federation had sales of over $500 million in 2001 and provides over 2 million farmer-members a living wage. Its members, both buffalo and cow farmers, are organized into village societies of roughly 200 farmers each. Using the slogan "A Taste of India," the cooperative has been able to capitalize on national pride, cater to local tastes, and capture significant market share from Unilever, Pizza Hut, Domino's, and other competitors in the ice cream, cheese, and pizza businesses. The cooperative undersells the foreign competition on most products by keeping advertising costs low (depending on word of mouth) and by using its control of the raw material to market every component (from cream to skim milk to curd).[60]

• Schwäbisch Hällisches Schwein (pork from Schwäbisch Hall) is a cooperative in southwest Germany established in 1988 with the goal of giving its members a better price for their pork. The group has grown from 8 members to 340 members and had a turnover of $20 million in 1999. Its farmers raise, slaughter, package, and market a regional pig breed rescued from extinction and suited to living outdoors year-round. The co–op markets within a 150-kilometer radius around Schwäbisch Hall, selling the product in roughly 100 hotels and 150 independent butchers, as well as one local supermarket chain with 70 stores.[61]

Farm Shops

• In the United Kingdom, where food production often takes place close to population centers, farm shop sales are growing more than 20 percent per year. Christies Farm Shop in Nottinghamshire, England, has begun a catering service and provides most of the meat, potatoes, and vegetables for a local school cafeteria.[62]

• AVEC (Agriculteurs en Vente Collective Direct), a farmers' cooperative in the Rhone-Alpes region of southwest France, runs 19 farm stores that offer a wide range of foods produced and processed on members' farms, including cheeses, wines, jams, sausages, fruits, and vegetables. One AVEC store reports roughly 2,000 customers each week and revenues of about $2 million each year, which are shared by 25 families on 10 farms.[63]

Schools

• In Florida, several dozen farmers got together and formed the New North Florida marketing cooperative in 1995 to process and market collard and turnip greens to schools. Today, the co–op is the main source of fruits and vegetables—

cut, sorted, packaged, and delivered shortly after harvest—for 30 schools in the area and greatly increases revenues to small-scale producers.[64]

• In Cornwall, England, the Cornwall County Council's in-house meal service provider is backing local food suppliers as part of a £1 million contract to supply school meals to 32 county primary and secondary schools. To date, three-year contracts, worth a total of approximately £350,000 a year, have been awarded to four local suppliers for fresh meat, frozen foods, and vegetables. "Everyone wins," says Ian Doble of Doble Quality Foods, the contractor for frozen food. "The schools and the children get high quality fresh food, the local economy gets a boost, and there are even fewer trucks journeying all over the country."[65]

• In 2000, the Italian government and several regional governments passed new laws obliging local authorities to include organic and locally produced ingredients in their school menus. There are now over 300 organic school meal services in Italy, and hundreds more local meal services. Officials and citizens pushed for this shift partly to reinforce the traditional Mediterranean diet, using more seasonal fruits and vegetables, less meat, and fewer processed foods. As part of this change, many schools are teaching more nutrition, cooking, and food selection skills, and incorporating visits to farms into their curricula.[66]

Restaurants and Institutional Buyers

• The University of North Iowa Local Food Project, initiated by the Center for Energy and Environmental Education at the university, worked with institutional food buyers (hospitals, nursing homes, colleges, restaurants, and groceries) in northeast Iowa to explore ways they could purchase a greater portion of their food from local farmers and food processors. Since 1998, the project's 10 participating institutions have spent nearly $600,000 of their food purchases locally. One local restaurant, Rudy's Tacos, now spends 71 percent of its food budget on fresh, locally grown ingredients.[67]

• "Buying locally tends to ensure that we get fresher product," said Josh Conrad, the marketing director for Casa

Nueva Restaurant and Cantina in Athens, Ohio, a worker-owned restaurant which buys 85 percent of its produce from 20 local farms and food businesses. Casa Nueva, which generated over $1 million in sales in 2000, has a goal of sourcing 100 percent of its produce locally in the next three years. Casa Nueva has recently developed Limited Harvest foods, a seasonal line of salsas, pickles, jams, and other packaged goods that are widely sold throughout Ohio.[68]

Consumer food cooperatives or buying clubs

• Japanese farmers sell about 60 percent of their produce directly to consumers, and at least half of that is sold to consumer groups or cooperatives. Most of these consumer groups were started by women concerned about the quality of their food or the high price of foods in conventional stores. The smaller groups might include 10 to 30 households working with a single farmer, while the nation's largest group has a membership of more than 200,000 households and is served by farmer networks all over Japan. There are now 800 to 1,000 of these groups in Japan, with a membership of roughly 11 million people and an annual turnover of over $15 billion.[69]

• In the northwestern United States, the Puget Consumers' Cooperative, which was started as a food buying club of 15 families in 1963, now has seven markets and 40,000 members, and is the largest natural food co-op in the nation, with $67 million in annual sales. The co-op supports dozens of area farmers and over 50 local food companies, producing everything from "microbrew tofu" and herbal teas to natural Oregon beef.[70]

• In Bristol, England, the Hartcliffe Health & Environment Action Group created the "Food for All Shop," a food cooperative formed to improve nutrition and bring together local growers and shoppers. Because the co-op is partly supported by the Bristol City Council, members only have to pay a small annual fee of £2. The co-op also keeps costs down by requiring members to volunteer time to work in the shop, and keeps prices down by marking up produce just enough to cover expenses. The co-op sources much of its fruits, vegetables, meat, and dairy products from local organic producers, and offers classes in cooking, nutrition, and gardening.[71]

A few important lessons come out of these successes. First, work together. Even in cases where there is interest in sourcing food locally, the difficulties can overwhelm the benefits. The people who buy foods for restaurants, hotels, caterers, supermarkets, cafeterias, and other institutions are used to the ease of ordering from one or two large wholesalers that can supply any product year-round. Groups of farmers that can employ someone as a broker or marketer will not only improve their own business prospects, but also make it more convenient for institutional kitchens to support local agriculture.[72]

Second, farmers and food businesses will need to ally with others to break into a highly consolidated market. For instance, unlike large supermarket chains or food manufacturers, most smaller ventures will not be able to launch massive advertising campaigns to promote their products. For them, getting the word out will depend on other strategies, including linking up with environmental groups, consumer groups, or other organizations sympathetic to the virtues of local foods. For example, Patchwork Family Farm, a Missouri (U.S.A.) cooperative of hog farmers that slaughters, packs, and markets its own meat, did much of its original marketing through rural church groups interested in the plight of family farms.[73]

Third, in marketing their wares locally, farmers and food businesses should capitalize on the many competitive advantages that they will always have over the industrial food system, including freshness, variety, detailed information on how the food was produced, and the opportunity to develop social bonds with their customers. Marketing surveys on the promotion of local foods have found that sales would benefit from piggybacking on related ecological or social distinctions, like "organic," "hormone-free," and "raised by family farmers." In contrast to the anonymity of food bought from a food conglomerate, farmers and others marketing local food should not take for granted the appeal of "food with a face"— food that has a unique and important story behind its creation. (See Box 3.)[74]

BOX 3

Fair Trade: Supporting the Local From Far Away

Given the economics of food trade, farmers growing food for export are often using land they might instead use to feed themselves, without getting adequate compensation for this sacrifice. Is there some way to maintain the close social connection between grower and eater over a long distance, to ensure that the eater is helping the local community to improve its livelihood?

Enter the fair trade movement. Just as buying direct from the farmer ensures that a greater share of the profits remains in the farmer's hands and in the local community, fair trade arrangements guarantee these results even for long-distance exchanges. Often a fair trade agreement requires that producers receive a price for their commodity that is a certain percentage higher than the price on the world market, or that the farmers and farmworkers have access to health and education benefits or the right to organize into unions and cooperatives. Fair trade coffee, chocolate, and other tropical exports are already on the market. One particularly innovative example involves the Day Chocolate Company, makers of fair trade chocolate bars sold widely in England. With the help of several charities and corporate sponsors, Kuapa Kokoo, a cooperative of over 40,000 Ghana cocoa growers, created the Day Chocolate Company and continue as one-third owners. Co-op members also sit on the board.

Source: See Endnote 74.

Fourth, given the growing public interest in eating local foods, some local food businesses are likely to enjoy substantial economic success. Yet this does not have to mean that they will grow away from their roots; several companies have shown that growth need not jeopardize an interest in being a continual source of jobs, income, and food for the local community. Company bylaws and linkages to the local foodshed can help keep the business locally owned and anchored. For instance, the farmer-members of Organic Valley, the largest organic dairy cooperative and the largest seller of organic dairy products in the United States, have made a commitment to "regional flavor" in their company mission by selling milk produced in a given region largely in that region. Organic Valley's new regional milk cartons—for instance, milk sold in the northeastern United States carries the label, "Grown by our Northeast farmers for Northeast consumers"—help solidify this connection for consumers and promote local foods.[75]

Rebuilding the Local Foodshed

The food system is now so intensely consolidated and support for long-distance food is so pervasive that the scattered
efforts to invigorate local food systems could have as little effect
as a mosquito bite on a tractor. Widespread change is not
likely to come without a healthy dose of political support.

Part of the argument for governments to give preferen-
tial treatment (such as local procurement laws or tax breaks)
to local farmers and food businesses is that the existence of a
healthy local foodshed yields benefits to society that are not
adequately represented in the price farmers get for selling
their crops or the price that consumers pay at the checkout
counter. In addition to being a source of fresh, ripe food, a local
farm can help halt the advance of sprawl and provide great aesthetic appeal. A mayor concerned about obesity among city residents might be interested in creating space for more farmers'
markets, knowing that they are likely to increase fruit and vegetable consumption. "Municipalities are continually creating
incentives for local real estate or mall development or even
sports complexes," says the University of Wisconsin's Kloppenburg, "but what about incentives for local food businesses,
community kitchens, or urban farming?"[76]

A relatively new institution popping up in states and
cities around the world that might help promote such policies
is the local food policy council. (See Box 4.) There are at least
15 local food policy councils in North America, and several more
cities and states are planning to create them. (The number of
local food policy councils outside of North America is less well
documented, but similar institutions exist around the world.)
The councils typically emerge out of informal coalitions of
local politicians, hunger activists, environmentalists, sustainable agriculture advocates, and community development interests, allowing food policy decisions to reflect a broad range of
interests and tap possible synergies. For instance, hunger
activists, senior citizens, and farmers might join to lobby for
farmers' market coupons that improve availability for hungry

BOX 4

Examples of Local Food Policy Councils and Their Achievements

The Hartford Food System (HFS), a nonprofit founded in 1978, works to give people in Connecticut better access to nutritious and affordable food. The group has helped establish farmers' markets, distribute coupons to low-income households for use at farmers' markets, improve public transportation to food outlets, create a grocery delivery service for homebound elderly people, and launch the Connecticut Food Policy Council, a body that helps guide Connecticut food policy. The group tracks prices at Hartford supermarkets, examines other food trends in Hartford and Connecticut, and operates a 400-member CSA that distributes 40 percent of its produce to low-income people. It also educates the public about farmland preservation and lobbies for policies that preserve farmland. HFS started a statewide farmland trust to preserve farmland in 2002.

Founded in 1998, Devon County Foodlinks helps build links between local farmers and food outlets in Devon County, England. On a annual budget of less than £500,000, this government-funded effort has created an estimated 150 new jobs, 15 farmers' markets, and 18 box (CSA) schemes. It has also spawned many successful food businesses and helped to retain an estimated £9 million in the local economy.

Herb Barbolet, director of Farm Folk/City Folk (FFCF) since it was founded in 1993, describes this non-profit group as "a catalyst for building webs and networks to support local foods in British Columbia." In addition to coordinating food delivery schemes and farmers' markets, FFCF has started a rooftop gardens project and opened a healthy café in inner-city areas of Vancouver, where good food options are limited. The group holds an annual "Feast of Fields" harvest festival that features local foods. FFCF has also converted some large city parks slated for development into working farms. As part of its Linking Land and Future Farmers project, FFCF acts as a matchmaker to link people with land who no longer actively farm it with people who want to farm but cannot afford to. Such links frequently bring together recent immigrants and retiring farmers without heirs.

In 1991 the City of Toronto created the Toronto Food Policy Council (TFPC), a body with representatives from food corporations, conventional and organic farms, co-operatives, unions, social justice and faith groups, and the city council. TFPC developed a "Field to Table" program to link low-income Toronto residents who need fresh produce with local farmers who have high quality vegetables to sell. TFPC helps broker business between local farmers and school food programs, food co-ops, and hospitals. It also helped develop a kitchen incubator for aspiring food businesses. TFPC has educated the public and lobbied politicians on issues ranging from farmland preservation and transportation design to food waste recovery and genetically modified foods.

Source: See Endnote 77.

citizens while increasing market outlets for farmers.[77]

These local councils might have another policy making advantage. "Only an entity on the ground that knows the community and knows the nuances of the local food system, knows how to make the system work for local folks," says Mark Winne of the Hartford Food System (HFS), a Connecticut food policy council. Policies designed in the rarefied air of bureaucracies may not be relevant or effective for specific cities or communities. HFS interviewed hundreds of low-income Hartford households to determine the main causes of hunger in the city. After finding a strong correlation between frequent bouts of hunger and poor access to transportation options, the group worked with city officials to modify existing bus lines so that routes connected low-income communities with existing supermarkets. HFS also helped to open several farmers' markets and a new supermarket in the same poorly served area.[78]

Edward Seidler, senior officer at the UN Food and Agriculture Organization's Marketing Group, suggests that city authorities consider establishing strategically placed local retail markets—along bus routes or near major business centers, for instance—that cater to low income consumers, while simultaneously providing outlets for farmers, especially those small farmers growing vegetables on city edges. (See Box 5.) As many Third World cities begin to erect housing developments and transportation infrastructure to accommodate their rapidly growing populations, local officials who fail to incorporate food shops and markets into their plans will confront masses of residents who have to pay extra and travel long distances to buy food.[79]

One of the more comprehensive food planning efforts comes from southwestern England, where Devon County Foodlinks has been working since 1998 to build links between local growers and local food outlets. This government-funded effort helps farmers diversify their crops and explore on-farm processing, sets up farmers' markets and box delivery schemes, provides grants for new local food businesses, and connects local growers to shops, pubs, restaurants, schools, and government institutions that regularly buy food. According to

BOX 5

How To Keep a City Fed

In their book *Hope's Edge*, Francis Moore Lappé and Anna Lappé chronicle the "new social mentality" around getting food to urbanites that took root in Belo Horizonte, Brazil's fourth-largest city, in 1993. According to the Lappés, Belo Horizonte, where one-fifth of the city's youngest children used to be malnourished, is "the only city...in the capitalist world that has decided to make food security a right of citizenship." The city serves four nutritious meals each day to all students at the city's schools, provides over 40 local farmers with space around town to set up stalls, established a "Green Basket" program linking hospitals, restaurants, and other big food buyers to local growers, and runs the Restaurante Popular (the people's restaurant), which serves over 4,000 meals a day at less than half the market price. The foundation of this effort is a network of 26 warehouse-sized stores around the city that sell local produce at fixed prices, often half the price charged by nearby grocers. These stores are located on prime urban real-estate that the city rents to entrepreneurs at rock-bottom prices. In exchange, the city reserves the right to set the price of produce and obligates the vendors to make weekend deliveries of produce to poor neighborhoods outside the city center.

The government helps to keep food affordable by improving the functioning of the market. For example, the city publicizes the prices of 45 basic foods at 40 supermarkets every week so that consumers know where to shop and when they're being gouged. The city has also set up a 20-member local food council to help form partnerships with church and labor groups and to advise the city on how it might further improve the local food system. Officials in Belo Horizonte see these efforts as cost effective because they know good nutrition benefits educational performance and public health. While economic dogma often discourages government intervention in markets, the experience of Belo Horizonte shows that local authorities can play an essential role in ensuring that the local food economy is functioning properly and serving the public interest.

Source: See Endnote 79.

---

founder Ian Hutchcroft, "our interest is in rural regeneration," a term that captures not only an interest in encouraging good land use, reducing food shipping, raising farm income, and creating jobs in food businesses, but also regenerating social ties throughout the community. (A large portion of the funding came from public health agencies interested in countering the rise of obesity and the fast-food culture.) "We are making 'interventions' to address local market failures," Hutchcroft notes, "because the private sector is not investing in local food businesses in a major way, and, in many ways, the cards are stacked against them." The Devon project has inspired similar efforts in six other counties in the Southwest and elsewhere in England, as well as projects scattered throughout Wales and Scotland.[80]

Because "the cards are stacked" against local food, financial and other incentives may be needed to help launch local food businesses. In 1993, for example, the Appalachian Center for Economic Networks (ACENet), partly supported by the U.S. Department of Agriculture, began converting an old lumberyard in Athens, Ohio, into a fully equipped and approved commercial kitchen that could be used as an incubator for local food entrepreneurs. ACENet now provides training in food processing, marketing, product development, and business management, in addition to pointing start-up processors to local sources for fruit, vegetables, meat, and dairy products. The kitchen is used by 300 specialty food businesses, and has spawned more than 120 start-ups and created hundreds of jobs. (The Herbal Sage Tea Company, The Dotty Baker, Cliffie's Salsa, and Integration Acres are just a few of the businesses that have now "graduated" from the kitchen incubator.) Toronto offers another example: the Food Policy Council there has argued for tax and zoning policies to encourage a small-scale food processing industry in the city, not only as a source of jobs but also to "source raw materials close to the homebase, thereby sustaining Ontario farms that help preserve Toronto's greenbelt."[81]

Governments can help boost demand for local food through procurement policies in their own cafeterias, a strategy that has been used to invigorate the market for a range of "alternative" products, from sustainably harvested lumber to energy-efficient light bulbs. Large purchases by government agencies (as well as by universities, schools, and restaurants) can provide the critical mass to encourage local food distribution networks that can then supply other local outlets as well. In the United Kingdom, planners in the towns of Eaton and Abbeystead have combined local-food procurement policies for schools, hotels, and food businesses with other policies to ensure that farming stays closely linked to community welfare, including low-interest loans for young and beginning farmers and limits on farm size and out-of-town farm ownership. The average age of a farmer in Abbeystead is 32, compared to a British average of almost 55, and average farm profitability is among the highest in the nation.[82]

In the United Kingdom, where a growing interest in local foods has forced major supermarkets to adapt their buying practices, a recent government commission recommended an interesting financial incentive: Retailers that "give over a portion of their store as an outlet for local producers to sell direct to the public should receive business rate [tax] relief on that part of their premises." Corporations can play the same role if they choose: Wegmans Food Markets, a supermarket chain in the United States, has a "Home Grown" program that gives preference to produce from local farmers when fresh food is in season. Under this program, Wegmans gives bonuses to produce managers who exceed a certain quota of produce from local growers (roughly 30 percent) because the chain knows that people will often pay more for local produce, and because local produce draws customers in to the store.[83]

Some of the strongest threats to local food systems are created at the national or international levels, and will require action there. (See Box 6, page 56.) Current international trade agreements restrict the ability of nations to protect and build domestic farm economies, forbidding domestic price supports, tariffs on imported goods, and preference for products based on place of origin. (The international free-trade community is up in arms about Japan's recent proclamation that it needs to "boost self-sufficiency," "protect its farmers," and "provide consumers with cheap, safe, fresh products *grown at home*.") At the same time, these agreements leave considerable wiggle room with respect to other self-serving forms of trade manipulation, including the ability of wealthy nations to dump subsidized crops on the world market—an economic weapon that can squash local food production by driving prices down and actually worsen poverty among those who depend on agriculture for their income. "The WTO and related trade agree-

BOX 6

National and International Policy Changes To Help Rebuild Local Foodsheds

- **Enforce antitrust legislation at the national and global levels.** As every link in the agribusiness chain consolidates, there is a dire need for national governments and international trade bodies to break up monopolies and oligopolies, and generally enforce antitrust legislation. In the face of widespread consolidation, collective bargaining by farmers and local food businesses will be essential, although several nations have laws that prevent such collective bargaining.

- **Eliminate commodity payments.** Today, most agricultural policy encourages the production of generic commodities, while actually discouraging farmers from producing food for local markets. A case in point is the more than $320 billion that governments of industrial nations spend each year to support agriculture. Since the lion's share of this money is tied to the production of a handful of commodities—such as corn, soybeans, and wheat—this arrangement discourages diversification. Farmers interested in diversifying out of the handful of crops that receive payments and getting into food processing jeopardize a significant source of income.

- **Restructure agricultural education, research, and extension.** Agricultural ministries, research centers, and universities should shift from an exclusive focus on production to a more integrated view of the whole farm business. Rich Pirog of the Leopold Center for Sustainable Agriculture at Iowa State University argues that people interested in rebuilding local and regional food systems "need to create new alliances at our universities with the Colleges of Business, not just the Colleges of Agriculture, since the business school has the expertise in marketing, distribution, and supply chains design."

- **Tax fossil fuels rather than subsidize them.** Long-distance food would be vastly more expensive if oil prices were to rise, something that many geologists and energy analysts argue could happen in the next decade or so as world oil production peaks. In the meantime, climate change—which will likely have direct effects on the stability of food production—provides the strongest argument for radically reducing fossil fuel use. National governments can accelerate this shift by eliminating existing subsidies for coal, oil, and natural gas and raising taxes on these same fossil fuels.

- **Eliminate food dumping and reform world trade rules to ensure food sovereignty.** Existing international trade rules prevent nations from safeguarding and developing domestic and local food production. Local labels, country-of-origin labeling, procurement policies, and quality standards are often seen as barriers to trade, but countries should have the power to determine what foods cross their borders, including the power to forbid imports of a given food during its domestic harvest season.

Source: See endnote 84.

ments close off countries from trying to pursue development strategies predicated on strong internal food markets," says Peter Rosset of FoodFirst/Institute for Agriculture and Development Policy, "a strategy that proved central to the economic growth in the United States in the 19th century and for the East Asian miracle economies and China after World War II."[84]

The Personal Case for Eating Local

The more communities forsake their food self-reliance, the harder it becomes to recapture this market from a food monopoly. The alarming pace at which local farms and food businesses are fading away indicates that the initiative of well-meaning government officials to support and protect local foods may simply not be enough.

A more diffuse, but potentially more powerful, entity may hold the key to the rebirth of local foodsheds: the food consumer. Socially and ecologically sound buying habits are not just the passive result of changes in the way food is produced, but can actually be the most powerful drivers of these changes. Among the range of simple actions that the average person can take to reinvigorate the local food economy are shopping at the local farmers' market, asking their favorite restaurant or food store to stock locally grown foods, and building a few weekly meals around seasonally available foods.[85] (See Box 7, page 58.)

Confronted with the notion that food choices have landscape-shaping and climate-changing implications, a consumer may ask, "What's wrong with getting my food from some distant land, if the food is cheap and the system works?" For most of us, the most convincing arguments for eating local will not include abstract concepts such as the tremendous energy use (and thus pollution) associated with hauling food across continents or the loss of crop diversity from consolidation in the food business. The most compelling arguments may instead be psychological and emotional—the realization that if we con-

BOX 7

What Individuals Can Do

What defines "local" food? Is it food from one's nation? From one's state or province? From farms within 50 kilometers of your house? When ecologist Gary Nabhan decided to eat locally for a year, he drew the line at 400 kilometers from his house, partly guided by the size of the watershed in which he lived. Nutritionist Joan Gussow suggests trying to buy food produced "within a day's leisurely drive of our homes," a goal "designed to maintain a living countryside." Regardless of the precise definition, there are several actions people can take to promote local food systems:

- Learn what foods are in season in your area and try to build your diet around them.

- Shop at a local farmers' market. People living in areas without a farmers' market might try to start one themselves, linking up with interested neighbors and friends and contacting nearby farmers and agricultural officials for help. People can do the same with CSA subscription schemes.

- Ask the manager or chef of your favorite restaurant how much of the food on the menu is locally grown, and then encourage him or her to source food locally. Urge that the share be increased. People can do the same at their local supermarket or school cafeteria.

- Take a trip to a local farm to learn what it produces.

- Host a harvest party at your home or in your community that features locally available and in-season foods.

- Produce a local food directory that lists all the local food sources in your area, including CSA arrangements, farmers' markets, food co-ops, restaurants emphasizing seasonal cuisine and local produce, and farmers willing to sell direct to consumers year-round.

- Buy extra quantities of your favorite fruit or vegetable when it is in season and experiment with drying, canning, jamming, or otherwise preserving it for a later date.

- Plant a garden and grow as much of your own food as possible.

- Speak to your local politician about forming a local food policy council to help guide decisions that affect the local foodshed.

Source: See endnote 85.

tinue on the present course, one day we will wake up to find that there are no locally owned farms, dairies, canneries, or grocers in sight, leaving us beholden to whatever farmer or food business is willing to ship us food on their terms.

This appears to explain what has happened in Britain, which in recent years has played host to an unfortunate series of food scares, from the discovery of mad cow disease and the recent outbreak of foot-and-mouth disease to ongoing concerns over genetically modified foods. These scares prompted British citizens to start asking where their food was coming from and instilled a wariness of long-distance food. The 2001 foot-and-mouth outbreak, which brought sales of British meat to an abrupt halt and devastated rural communities, was exacerbated by long-distance food transportation; it spread considerably farther and faster than an earlier outbreak in 1967, largely because animals today are shipped from all over the nation to central slaughterhouses. In 1967 most slaughtering and consumption took place locally. (Investigation also showed that the infectious animal feed for the recent outbreak came from China.)[86]

Many British consumers have restructured their food buying habits in the wake of the scares, flocking to farmers' markets and subscribing to box (CSA) schemes, seeking out food with some human connection that they can trust. Marsha Bushwood of Promar International, a U.K.-based food consulting firm, points to surveys of consumers showing "a very strong desire to put their money directly in the hand of the farmer, due to growing concerns about food safety and due to growing cynicism about the motivations of agribusiness." Consumers seem to feel that the farmer is less likely to cheat them than a supermarket or a fast food chain, according to Bushwood. And the ability to interact with the person who knows how the crop or animal has been treated throughout its entire life has become particularly valuable, a sort of premium in an otherwise anonymous food system.[87]

In food industry jargon, this premium is known as "traceability," and it depends to a large extent on shortening the chain between the farmer and the eater. Bushwood notes that British supermarkets, concerned about loss of market share, are scrambling to host local food days in their stores, feature talks by local farmers, and even hold mock farmers' markets in their parking lots. (The Waitrose chain recently rolled out the slogan, "No other supermarket knows each of their milk producers.") A government report from 2002 predicted that "local food will enter the mainstream in the next few years," and noted that several supermarket retailers "see local food as the next major development in food retailing."[88]

This search for security and confidence is, of course, not limited to British consumers. Recent terrorist incidents have raised fears, especially in the United States, about how vulnerable a highly centralized and long-distance food system could be to tampering and disruption. (One estimate suggests that most major cities in the eastern United States have less than two days' supply of food on hand and are thus vulnerable to sudden transportation restrictions.) Food that spends large amounts of time in transit, changes hands multiple times, and is processed in huge batches provides nearly unlimited opportunities for both accidental and malicious contamination, on a scale impossible with a shorter, more decentralized food chain. (Small, local processing plants are not immune to such errors, accidents, or sabotage, although their scale would help limit the consequences.)[89]

Still, it would be inaccurate to view the case of Britain, or other places where people are increasingly interested in eating local, as simply a story about people driven by fear and paranoia. Many Brits, though first prompted by concerns about food safety, have now learned that local food is not only less susceptible to corruption of the food chain, but is also cheaper, tastier, and more pleasurable.

Carlo Petrini, founder and president of the Slow Food Movement ("a movement for the protection of the right to taste") notes that the price societies have paid for having access to every possible food at any time of year is "the deliberate development of species with characteristics functional only to the food industry and not to the pleasure of food, and the consequent sacrifice of many varieties and breeds on the altar of mass-production." Petrini argues, for instance, that we've lost the tastiest, juiciest fruits because they couldn't be transported or it cost too much to process them, and crop breeders have instead developed varieties able to withstand the rigors of shipping and mechanical harvesting. (In the United

States—a global leader in long-distance food—more than half of all tomatoes are harvested and shipped green, and then artificially ripened upon arrival at their final destination.) People around the world have traditionally relished the excitement of eating foods at their peak of flavor and ripeness, says Petrini, an excitement reinforced by an intimate knowledge of food seasons and an array of harvest festivals. While skeptics might view such seasonal cuisine as constraining, Petrini considers it "much more of a constraint to be forced to eat standardized, tasteless industrial food products full of preservatives and artificial flavorings," often of substandard quality because they are rarely in season.[90]

If the pleasures of taste (and double-blind studies have shown that farmers' market produce consistently trumps supermarket fare in this category) seem to be a rather selfish argument in favor of local food, consider the constellation of meaningful human connections that emerge from the local foodshed, in contrast to the anonymity and coldness of supermarkets, packaged foods, and fast-food joints. Slow Food, now with 75,000 members in 80 nations, views these social interactions between citizens and bakers, butchers, and farmers, as well as meals shared with friends and family, as inseparable from the joy of eating locally. During his year-long experiment in digging deeper into his foodshed and eating only food raised within 400 kilometers of his home—compared with a typical American diet whose components often come from thousands of kilometers away—ecologist Gary Nabhan made dozens of new friends. For urbanites, in particular, local food might also provide one of the few remaining connections to nature, rural ways, rural people, and an awareness of what is happening to our food supply. (Margaret Mead suggested that food might be our most intimate connection to "the whole problem of the pollution and exhaustion of our environment.")[91]

Perhaps the most persuasive case for eating local is the high level of control that it gives us over the food we eat. As decisionmaking in the food chain grows ever more distant and concentrated—confined behind fewer corporate doors—the ability of the average person to know and influence what is going into the food supply shrinks accordingly. A case in point is the burgeoning field of genetically modified organisms. A coalition that disingenuously calls itself the Alliance for Better Foods—made up of large food retailers, food processors, biotech companies, and corporate-financed farm organizations—has launched a $50 million public "educational" campaign, in addition to giving hundreds of thousands of dollars to U.S. lawmakers and political parties, to head off the mandatory labeling of such foods. In contrast to such backroom dealing, farmers markets, CSA arrangements, and locally owned food businesses all tend to return decision-making power to the local community. Local food access options mean that consumers who want meat raised without hormones and antibiotics have a good chance of finding a farmer nearby who can deliver. Direct feedback to the farmer means an immediate response to personal preferences.[92]

People who aim to take back this control will quickly realize that it will not come easily. We are increasingly removed from our food, not just by distance, but also by process—by the chopping, cooking, coloring, flavoring, and other forms of processing that transform the raw material harvested from the soil into packaged food. Especially in the developed world, as more meals come out of boxes, cans, or Styrofoam containers, more and more people no longer know (or have never known) how to cook, preserve foods (through canning, pickling, or drying), garden, or identify wild edible plants—skills that were essential to the survival of many people only a couple of generations ago.[93]

This is not to say that everyone will go back to canning, and the long work hours and commute times of modern life do not always leave time to enjoy a homecooked meal. But there can be great pleasure and independence in relearning these forgotten arts. People who participate in CSA arrangements often report that they are forced to be creative and resourceful cooks, shaping dishes around the seasons and evolving into competent soup makers to take advantage of leftover and surplus foods. Growing, harvesting, selecting, preserving, and cooking food in the comfort of one's home also provides an ideal opportunity for interaction between parents and children.[94]

JoAnn Jaffe, a sociologist at the University of Regina, Canada, argues that the loss of food skills weakens consumer sovereignty, increasing the capacity of food manufacturers and retailers to manipulate tastes and buying behaviors, and making it possible to introduce "an endless stream of packaged, processed, and industrially transformed foodstuffs." Jaffe suggests a retaliatory strategy of "eating lower on the marketing chain" by buying food as locally as possible in order to regain sovereignty and control. Eating lower on the marketing chain will often be healthier, because buying more food direct generally means eating more fresh fruits and vegetables, and because many of the extra steps between the farmer and the consumer remove nutrients and fiber and add fat, sugar, salt, and other fillers.[95]

Buying locally can even save money, and not just because raw ingredients are often less expensive—per unit of nutrition delivered—than prepared, packaged foods. In some cases—particularly in inner-city food deserts and other communities where food options are limited—local food will be less expensive. In one survey, food sold at farmers' markets and through a food delivery scheme in southwest England—fruits, vegetables, meat, eggs, and certified organic products—was on average 30 to 40 percent cheaper than products of similar quality from the local supermarket. (In many cases, the supermarkets did not carry the same in-season produce found at the farmers market.) For $375, the Food Bank Farm in Hadley, Massachusetts, will deliver produce that would cost $800 at a supermarket and as much as $1,200 at an upscale gourmet store. Fadzavanhu Enterprises, the local peanut butter maker in Zimbabwe, undersells multinational competitors like Cairns Foods by as much as 15 percent.[96]

These individual actions may seem small and disconnected, even futile. Not so: every successful effort around the world to rebuild a local foodshed ultimately began with the work of an individual or small group. Four housewives started Fadzavanhu Enterprises; it now provides a market for many local farmers and is seriously challenging the dominant, foreign-owned peanut butter brands in local stores. Organic Valley, the farmer-owned dairy cooperative that is now the largest seller of organic dairy products in the United States, was started 15 years ago by a handful of organic farmers in the Midwest. And the thousands of consumer cooperatives in Japan, which now include roughly 11 million members and buy over $15 billion of produce each year directly from Japanese farmers, were almost all started by housewives concerned about pesticides on their families' food and high prices in the supermarkets.

Whether one is a farmer, restaurateur, politician, banker, entrepreneur, student looking for a career, or concerned parent, there are an infinite number of entry points into the local food economy. The potential—and the need—for rebuilding local foodsheds is vast. But the work will always depend on motivated individuals searching for a more secure livelihood, a stronger community, or simply a delicious meal.

Organizations Working To Rebuild Local Foodsheds

Policymaking Organizations

CityNet
5-F International Organizations
Centre
1-1-1 Minato-Mirai – Nishi-ku
Yokohama 220-0012
Japan
tel: +81-45- 223-2161
fax: +81-45-223-2162
e-mail: info@citynet-ap.org
website:
www.CityNet-ap.org/en/index.html

*International Union of Local
   Authorities*
IULA World Secretariat
PO Box 90646
2509 LP The Hague
The Netherlands
tel: +31-70-306-6066
fax: +31-70-350-0496
e-mail: iula@iula.org
website: www.iula.org

*International Council for Local
   Environmental Initiatives (ICLEI)*
World Secretariat
City Hall, West Tower 16th Floor
100 Queen Street, West
Toronto, Ontario M5H 2N2
Canada
tel: 416-392-1462
fax: 416-392-1478
e-mail: iclei@iclei.org
website: www.iclei.org

*World Federation of United Cities
   (FMCU-UTO)*
60 rue La Boétie
75008 Paris
France
tel: +33-1-53-96-05-80
fax: +33-1-53-96-05-81

e-mail: contact@fmcu-uto.org
website: www.fmcu-uto.org

Food and Agriculture Research Organizations

Center for Rural Affairs
101 S. Tallman St.
PO Box 406
Walthill, NE 68067
tel: 402-846-5428
fax: 402-846-5420
e-mail: info@cfra.org
website: www.cfra.org

Community Food Security Coalition
PO Box 209
Venice, CA 90294
tel: 310-822-5410
fax: 310-822-1440
e-mail: cfsc@foodsecurity.org
website: www.foodsecurity.org

*Henry A. Wallace Center for
   Agricultural and Environmental
   Policy at Winrock International*
1621 North Kent St., Suite 1200
Arlington, VA 22209-2134
tel: 703-525-9430
website: www.winrock.org

*International Society for Ecology
   and Culture*
Foxhole, Dartington
Devon TQ9 6EB
United Kingdom
tel: +44-180-386-8650
fax: +44-180-386-8651
e-mail: info@isec.org.uk
website: www.isec.org.uk

*Food First/Institute for Food and
   Development Policy*
398 60th Street
Oakland, CA 94618

tel: 510-654-4400
fax: 510-654-4551
e-mail: foodfirst@foodfirst.org
website: www.foodfirst.org

*Institute for Agriculture and
   Trade Policy*
2105 First Avenue South
Minneapolis, MN 55404
tel: 612-870-0453
fax: 612-870-4846
e-mail: iatp@iatp.org
website: www.iatp.org

Groups Working With Farmers To Build Marketing and Processing Capacity, and Make Connections to Consumers

Assocation for Better Land Husbandry
PO Box 39042
Nairobi
Kenya
tel: + 25-4-2-521-090
e-mail: jcheatle@net2000ke.com
website: www.ablh.org

*Intermediate Technology Development
   Group*
Bourton Hall
Bourton-on-Dunsmore
Rugby CV23 9QZ
United Kingdom
tel: +44-192-663-4400
fax: +44-192-663-4401
e-mail: itdg@itdg.org.uk
website: www.itdg.org

*Appropriate Technology Transfer
   for Rural Areas*
PO Box 3657
Fayetteville, AR 72702
tel: 800-346-9140
website: www.attra.org

Food Circles Networking Project
Department of Rural Sociology
University of Missouri at Columbia
204 Gentry

Columbia, MO 65211
tel: 573-882-3776
fax: 573-882-5127
e-mail: HendricksonM@missouri.edu
website:
www.foodcircles.missouri.edu

*Leopold Center for Sustainable
   Agriculture*
Iowa State University
209 Curtiss Hall
Ames, IA 50011-1050
tel: 515-294-3711
fax: 515-294-9696
e-mail: leocenter@iastate.edu
website: www.leopold.iastate.edu

Groups Promoting Local Food

Hartford Food System
509 Wethersfield Ave.
Hartford, CT 06114
tel: 860-296-9325
fax: 860-296-8326
e-mail: info@hartfordfood.org
website: www.hartfordfood.org

*ANDES (Association for Nature
   Conservation and Sustainable
   Development/Kechua-Aymara Asso-
   ciation for Sustainable Livelihoods)*
Apartado 567
Cuzco
Perú
tel: +51-84-245-021
e-mail: andes@andes.org.pe
website: www.andes.org.pe

Slow Food
Via Mendicità 8
12042 Bra (CN)
Italy
tel: +39-172-419-611
e-mail: international@slowfood.com
website: www.slowfood.com

Farm Folk/City Folk Society
106–131 Water Street
Vancouver, BC V6B 4M3

Canada
tel: 604-730-0450
fax: 604-730-0451
e-mail: office@ffcf.bc.ca
website: www.ffcf.bc.ca

*Sustain: The Alliance for Better Food
    and Farming*
94 White Lion Street
London N1 9PF
United Kingdom
tel: +44-171-837-1228
fax: +44-171-837-1141
e-mail: sustain@sustainweb.org
website: www.sustainweb.org

Foundation for Local Food Initiatives
PO Box 1234
Bristol BS99 2PG
United Kingdom
tel: +44-845-458-9525
e-mail: mail@localfood.org.uk
website: www.localfood.org.uk

Vermont Fresh Network
116 State Street
Montpelier, VT 05620-2901
tel: 802-229-4706
fax: 802-229-2200
e-mail: info@vermontfresh.net
website: www.vermontfresh.net

Toronto Food Policy Council
277 Victoria Street, Suite 203
Toronto, Ontario M5B 1W1
Canada
tel: 416-338-7937
fax: 416-392-1357
e-mail: tfpc@city.toronto.on.ca
website: www.city.toronto.on.ca/
health/tfpc_index.htm

FoodRoutes Network
PO Box 443
Millheim, PA 16854
tel: 814-349-6000

fax: 814-349-2280
website: www.foodroutes.org

Urban Agriculture Groups

Just Food
307 7th Ave., Suite 120
New York, NY 10001
tel: 212-645-9880
fax: 212-645-9881
e-mail: info@justfood.org
website: www.justfood.org

*City Farmer, Canada's Office of
    Urban Agriculture*
#801-318 Homer St.
Vancouver, BC V6B 2V3
Canada
tel: 604-685-5832
fax: 604-685-0431
e-mail: cityfarm@interchange.ubc.ca
website: www.cityfarmer.org

The Urban Agriculture Network
4701 Connecticut Ave, NW
Washington, DC 20008
tel: 202-362-5095
e-mail: urbanag@compuserve.com

Notes

1.   Matthew Hora, Capital Area Food Bank, discussion with author, 20 February 2002.

2.   Ibid.; Matthew Hora and Judy Tick, *From Farm to Table: Making the Connection in the Mid-Atlantic Food System* (Washington, D.C.: Capital Area Food Bank, 2001). For a description of the aggressive marketing of produce from California see Steven Stoll, *The Fruits of Natural Advantage: Making the Industrial Countryside in California* (Berkeley: University of California Press, 1998).

3.   Hora, op. cit. note 1; Hora and Tick, op. cit. note 2.

4.   Trade value and volume from United Nations Food and Agriculture Organization, *FAOSTAT Statistics Database*, at <http://apps.fao.org>, updated 4 July 2002.

5.   Farmland protection from "Suburban Harvest," *Preservation*, January/February 2002, pp. 55-61, 87; Accokeek Ecosystem Farm from Shane LaBrake, manager of Ecosystem Farm, Accokeek, Maryland, discussion with author, 18 September 2002.

6.   Conversations at farmers' markets from Robert Sommer et al., "The Behavioral Ecology of Supermarkets and Farmers' Markets," *Journal of Environmental Psychology*, Vol. 1, March 1981, pp. 13-19, and more recent, unpublished studies from Robert Sommer, discussion with author, 23 February 2002; Bernadine Prince, director, FreshFarm Market, discussion with author, 29 July 2002; Elizabeth Becker, "19 Million Pounds of Meat Recalled After 19 Fall Ill," *New York Times*, 20 July 2002.

7.   Number of new farmers' markets and status of Anacostia greengrocer from Tosha Thompson, executive director, Community Harvest, Washington, D.C., discussion with author, 3 September 2002; description of Anacostia farmers' market from Hora, op. cit. note 1.

8.   Information on Tuscarora Organic Growers Cooperative from Chris Fullerton, manager, Tuscarora Organic Growers Cooperative, Hustontown, Pennsylvania, discussion with author, 3 August 2002; Nora Poullion, Restaurant Nora, discussion with author, 13 December 2001.

9.   Gary Paul Nabhan, *Coming Home to Eat: The Pleasures and Politics of Local Foods* (New York: W.W. Norton, 2002), p. 14.

10.   United Nations Food and Agriculture Organization, op. cit. note 4. Trade data have been adjusted for inflation using U.S. implicit GNP price deflator, U.S. Commerce Department, Bureau of Economic Analysis, <www.bea.doc.gov/bea/dn/ st-tabs.htm>, revised 29 August 2002.

11. United States surveys from Hora and Tick, op. cit. note 2, and Rich Pirog et al., *Food, Fuel, and Freeways: An Iowa Perspective on How Far Food Travels, Fuel Usage, and Greenhouse Gas Emissions* (Ames, Iowa: Leopold Center for Sustainable Agriculture, Iowa State University, 2001), pp. 1, 2; British statistics from Andy Jones, *Eating Oil: Food Supply in a Changing Climate* (London: Sustain, 2001), pp. 1, 10, 14, 30, 31.

12. Advances in refrigeration and transportation from William Coyle and Nicole Ballenger (eds.), *Technological Changes in the Transportation Sector: Effects on U.S. Food and Agricultural Trade, A Proceedings* (Washington, D.C.: Economic Research Service, United States Department of Agriculture, October 2000), pp. 33, 51, 52; refrigerated railroad cars from William Cronon, *Nature's Metropolis: Chicago and the Great West* (New York: W.W. Norton & Co., 1991), pp. 233, 234; ripening techniques from Norman N. Potter and Joseph H. Hotchkiss, *Food Science* (New York: Chapman & Hall, 1995), pp. 163-99; falling cost of shipping from Jones, op. cit. note 11, p. 20.

13. Sidney Mintz, "How Juice Went From Stone Age to Ice Age," *Wall Street Journal*, 22 June 2000, and Potter and Hotchkiss, op. cit. note 12, pp. 432-44.

14. Joan Gussow, *This Organic Life: Confessions of a Suburban Homesteader* (White River Junction, Vermont: Chelsea Green Publishing Company, 2001), p. 82; lettuce from David Pimentel, Cornell University, e-mail to author, 20 March 2002; lettuce to the United Kingdom from Jones, op. cit. note 11, p. 1; perishables from Stavros Evangelakakis, Cargolux, quoted in press release from "Fresh Opportunities: A Conference for Everyone Seeking a Share in This Fast Expanding Trade," Perishables Transportation Conference, 30 June-2 July 2002, Vitoria, Spain.

15. Annika Carlsson-Kanyama, "Climate Change and Dietary Choices: How Can Emissions of Greenhouse Gases From Food Consumption Be Reduced," *Food Policy*, Fall/Winter 1998, pp. 288, 289; emissions related to food transportation from Policy Commission on the Future of Farming and Food, *Food & Farming: A Sustainable Future*, (London: January 2002), p. 92; available at <www.cabinet-office.gov.uk/farming>.

16. Caroline Lucas, *Stopping the Great Food Swap: Relocalising Europe's Food Supply* (London: The Greens/European Free Alliance and European Parliament, 2001); Herman E. Daly, "The Perils of Free Trade," *Scientific American*, November 1993, pp. 50-57.

17. Jerry Goldstein, editor and publisher of *Biocycle: The Journal of Composting and Recycling*, discussion with author, 16 April 2002; for food waste success stories, see *Biocycle*, various issues, <www.jgpress.com/biocycle.htm>; growth in food packaging from Robert Pagan and Marguerite Lake, "A Whole-Life Approach to Sustainable Food Production," *UNEP Industry and Environment*, April-September 1999, pp. 16, 17; one-third from Kameshwari Pothukuchi and Jerome L. Kaufman, "Placing the Food System on the Urban Agenda: The Role of Municipal Institutions in Food Systems Planning," *Agriculture and Human*

Values, Vol. 16, Number 2, 1999, p. 217.

18. Ken Meter and John Rosales, *Finding Food in Farm Country: The Economics of Food & Farming in Southeast Minnesota* (Lanesboro, Minnesota: Community Design Center, 2001), pp. 3-5.

19. Distribution of the farm dollar in the United States from Stewart Smith, Department of Resource Economics and Policy, University of Maine, Orono, Maine, unpublished data sent to author, 4 February 2002.

20. Ken Belson, "Wal-Mart Dips $46 Million Toe Into Vast Japanese Economy," *New York Times*, 15 March 2002; Box 1 from the following: Hope Shand's analysis from Pat Roy Mooney, "Concentration in Corporate Power," *Development Dialogue* (Dag Hammarskjöld Centre, Uppsala, Sweden), January 2001, pp. 89, 90; pesticide and seed market from "Globalization, Inc., Concentration in Corporate Power: The Unmentioned Agenda," *Communique* (Winnipeg, Manitoba: ETC Group, 5 September 2001); vegetable seeds from "The Gene Giants: Update on Consolidation in the Life Industry," *Communique* (Winnipeg, Manitoba: Rural Advancement Foundation International [now ETC Group], 30 March 1999); trade statistics and retailers in Europe from Fileman Torres et al., "Agriculture in the Early XXI Century: Agrodiversity and Pluralism as a Contribution to Address Issues on Food Security, Poverty, and Natural Resource Conservation" (draft) (Rome: Global Forum on Agricultural Research, April 2000), p. 14; chicken purchases in Central America and retail sector in Brazil from William Vorley and Julio Berdegué, "The Chains of Agriculture," World Summit on Sustainable Development Opinion (London: IIED, May 2001) and Belson, op. cit. this note; beef and pork packing from William Heffernan, University of Missouri (Columbia), "Consolidation in the Food and Agriculture System," Report to the National Farmers Union, 5 February 1999; Hong Kong retail from Tim Lang, Thames Valley University, London, discussion with author, 14 June 2001.

21. David Seddon, University of Norwich, United Kingdom, discussion with author, 23 April 2002; export-oriented strategies from John Walton and David Seddon, *Free Markets and Food Riots: The Politics of Global Adjustment* (Oxford: Blackwell Publishers, May 1994), and Peter Uvin, *The International Organization of Hunger* (London: Kegan Paul International, 1994), pp. 92-128.

22. Uvin, op. cit. note 21.

23. Tim Weiner, "Corn Growing in Mexico 'Has Basically Collapsed' as U.S. Imports Flood Country," *New York Times*, 26 February 2002; United Nations Food and Agriculture Organization, op. cit. note 4.

24. Seddon, op. cit. note 21; Global Trade Watch, *Down on the Farm: NAFTA's Seven-Years War on Farmers and Ranchers in the U.S., Canada, and Mexico* (Washington, D.C.: Public Citizen, June 2001).

25. Lori Ann Thrupp et al., *Bittersweet Harvests for Global Supermarkets: Chal-

lenges in Latin America's Agricultural Export Boom (Washington, D.C.: World Resources Institute, April 1995), and quote from Lori Ann Thrupp, Environmental Protection Agency, discussion with author, 4 April 2002; evidence from Africa comes from Catherine Dolan et al., "Horticulture Commodity Chains: The Impact of the U.K. Market on the African Fresh Vegetable Industry," IDS Working Paper 96, Institute of Development Studies, University of Sussex, 1999; Global Trade Watch, op. cit. note 24.

26. New Economics Foundation, "Local Food Better for Rural Economy than Supermarket Shopping" (press release), London, United Kingdom, 7 August 2001.

27. West Africa from Christopher Delgado et al., "Agricultural Growth Linkages in Sub-Saharan Africa," IFPRI Research Report 107 (Washington, D.C.: International Food Policy Research Institute, December 1998), p. xii; Japan, South Korea, and Taiwan from Peter Rosset, "The Multiple Functions and Benefits of Small Farm Agriculture," Policy Brief No. 4 (Oakland, California: Food First/Institute for Food and Development Policy, September 1999), pp. 12, 13; Peter Rosset, Food First/Institute for Food and Development Policy, discussion with author, 21 January 2002.

28. Wendell Berry, "A Return to the Local: You Stay Home Too," *World Watch*, September/October 2000, p. 33.

29. Observers have noted that the giant swath of the United States devoted to corn isn't healthy for humans or the environment; sustaining this vast monoculture requires frequent doses of chemicals, and food businesses awash with cheap corn transform the crop into soda, fatty meat, and an array of other unhealthy products. See Michael Pollan, "When a Crop Becomes King," *New York Times*, 19 July 2002. Becky Tarbotton, International Society for Ecology and Culture, Devon, United Kingdom, discussion with author, 3 May 2002, and Katy Mamen, ISEC, Berkeley, California, discussion with author, 20 May 2002.

30. Alejandro Argumedo, ANDES, Cuzco, Peru, e-mail to author, 15 March 2002.

31. P. Mader et al., "Soil Fertility and Biodiversity in Organic Farming," *Science*, 31 May 2002; J.P. Reganold et al., "Sustainability of Three Apple Production Systems, *Nature*, 19 April 2001; Peter B. Reich et al., "Plant Diversity Enhances Ecosystem Responses to Elevated CO_2 and Nitrogen Deposition," *Nature*, 12 April 2001; and L.E. Drinkwater et al., "Legume-Based Cropping Systems Have Reduced Carbon and Nitrogen Losses," *Nature*, 26 November 1998.

32. Northwood Farms from Anja Lyngbaek, International Society for Ecology and Culture, Devon, United Kingdom, discussion with author, 5 June 2002.

33. Andy Jones, "An Environmental Assessment of Food Supply Chains: A Case Study on Dessert Apples," *Environmental Management*, forthcoming, draft sent to author 20 August 2002; United Nations Food and Agriculture Organization, op. cit. note 4.

34. Phil R. Kaufman, "Rural Poor Have Less Access to Supermarkets, Large Grocery Stores," *Rural Development Perspectives*, April 1999, pp. 19-26; Doug O'Brien quoted in Kerr Center for Sustainable Agriculture, "Hunger in the Heartland," *Field Notes* (newsletter), Winter 2001, p. 3.

35. Food deserts in rural areas from Claire Hinrichs, Department of Sociology, Iowa State University, Ames, Iowa, e-mail to author 4 September 2002; rise in obesity from Barry M. Popkin, "The Nutrition Transition and Its Health Implications in Lower-Income Countries," *Public Health Nutrition*, Vol. 1, Number 1, 1998, pp. 5-21.

36. Indigenous populations from Popkin, op. cit. note 35, and Carol Ballew et al., "Intake of Nutrients and Food Sources of Nutrients Among the Navajo: Findings From the Navajo Health and Nutrition Survey," *Journal of Nutrition*, October 1997, pp. 2085S-2093S; Oodham Indians from Maya Tauber and Andy Fisher, "A Guide to Community Food Projects," Community Food Security Coalition, Venice, California, 2000, pp. 2-3; Nabhan, op. cit. note 9, pp. 247, 260, 289-300.

37. Christian Peters et al., "Vegetable Consumption, Dietary Guidelines, and Agricultural Production in New York State: Implications for Local Food Economies," Department of Applied Economics and Management, Cornell University, Ithaca, New York, May 2002.

38. United Nations Food and Agriculture Organization, "Feeding Asian Cities," Proceedings of the Regional Seminar, Food Supply and Distribution to Cities Programme, Bangkok, Thailand, 27-30 November 2000.

39. United Nations Development Programme (UNDP), *Urban Agriculture: Food, Jobs and Sustainable Cities* (New York, 1996), p. 26, and Jac Smit, the Urban Agriculture Network, Washington, D.C., discussion with author, 13 August 2002. Box 2 from the following sources: historical sources from Luc J.A. Mougeot, "Urban Food Production: Evolution, Official Support, and Significance (with Special Reference to Africa)," Cities Feeding People Series, Report 8, International Development Research Centre, Ottawa, Canada, 1994, <www.city farmer.org/lucTOC26.html>; roof gardens in Vancouver from Collin Varner and Christine Allen, *Gardens of Vancouver* (Vancouver: Raincoast Book Distributors, 2000), and in Bogotá from Jac Smit and Joe Nasr, "Urban Agriculture for Sustainable Cities: Using Wastes and Idle Land and Water Bodies as Resources," *Environment and Urbanization*, Vol. 4, No. 2, 1992, pp. 141-51; Calcutta from United Nations Development Programme, *Urban Agriculture: Food, Jobs and Sustainable Cities* (New York, 1996), p. 187; Eduardo Spiaggi, "Urban Agriculture and Local Sustainable Development: The Integration of Economic, Social, Technical, and Environmental Variables in Rosario, Argentina," presented at International Development Research Centre Agropolis Awardee Conference, Ottawa, Canada, 26 March 2002; UNDP estimates from

United Nations Development Program, op. cit. this note, p. 26; Dar-Es-Salaam from Luc J.A. Mougeot, "Farming In and Around Cities," <www.world-bank.org/html/ fpd/urban/urb_age/urb_agri.doc>, viewed 17 September 2002, and Stefan Dongus, "Vegetable Production on Open Spaces in Dar-Es-Salaam: Spatial Changes from 1992 to 1999," Urban Vegetable Promotion Project, Dar-Es-Salaam, Tanzania, January 2000, <www.cityfarmer.org/daressalaam.htm>; Bamako from Isabel Maria Madaleno, "Cities of the Future: Urban Agriculture in the Third Millennium," *Food, Nutrition, and Agriculture*, Vol. 29, 2001, p. 17; nutrition studies from Daniel Maxwell, "Alternative Food Security Strategies: A Household Analysis of Urban Agriculture in Kampala," *World Development*, Vol. 23, No. 10, 1995, pp. 1669-81; Asian examples from United Nations Food and Agriculture Organization, op. cit. note 38, p. 16; Belém from Madaleno, op. cit. this note, pp. 18, 19; Cuba from Nelso Companioni et al., "The Growth of Urban Agriculture," in Fernando Funes et al. (eds.), *Sustainable Agriculture and Resistance: Transforming Food Production in Cuba*, (Oakland, California: Food First Books, 2002), pp. 227-29; St. Petersburg from Alexander Gavrilov, agriculture director of the Center for Citizen Initiatives, St. Petersburg, Russia, "Rooftop Gardening in St. Petersburg, Russia," <www.city farmer.org/russiastp.html>, 1 December 2001; Lisbon and London from Madaleno, op. cit. this note, pp. 15, 16; American food production in metropolitan areas from A.A. Sorenson et al., *Farming on the Edge* (DeKalb, Illinois: American Farmland Trust, 1997), <www.farmlandinfo.org/cae/foe2>, p. 5; Toronto community gardens from Wayne Roberts, project co-ordinator, Toronto Food Policy Council, discussion with author, 23 May 2002; Toronto rooftop garden from Lauren Baker, "Warehouse Rooftop Supports Urban Agriculture," *In Business*, March/April 2000, pp. 16-18.

40. Companioni et al., op. cit. note 39, pp. 220-36.

41. Pothukuchi and Kaufman, op. cit. note 17, pp. 213-24, and United Nations Food and Agricultural Organization, op. cit. note 38, p. 1.

42. Local food as best option for feeding poor urbanites from Pothukuchi and Kaufman, op. cit. note 17, p. 214; food expenses and options for poor urbanites from United Nations Food and Agriculture Organization, op. cit. note 45, p. 11, and Suzi Leather, *The Making of Modern Malnutrition* (London: The Caroline Walker Trust, 1996); supermarkets leaving inner cities from Frances Moore Lappé et al., *World Hunger: 12 Myths* (New York: Grove Press, 1998), p. 102.

43. Roberts, op. cit. note 39.

44. Argumedo, op. cit. note 30.

45. Emphasis on commodity production from Jules Pretty, University of Essex, United Kingdom, discussion with author, 23 February 2002, and Henry A. Wallace Center for Agricultural & Environmental Policy at Winrock International, *Making Changes: Turning Local Vision into National Solutions* (Winrock International: Arlington, Virginia, May 2001), p. 26; barriers to local food businesses from Policy Commission on the Future of Farming and Food, op cit.

note 15, p. 44; lack of entrepreneurial emphasis in developing world from Jules Pretty and Rachel Hine, *Reducing Food Poverty with Sustainable Agriculture: A Summary of New Evidence* (Colchester, U.K.: SAFE-World Research Project, University of Essex, February 2001), pp. 10, 17, and Sue Azam-Ali, International Technology Development Group, London, United Kingdom, discussion with author, 30 April 2002.

46. These American statistics refer only to markets registered with state governments, and officials speculate that there are probably thousands of additional unofficial ones. Timothy Egan, "Growers and Shoppers Crowd Farmers' Markets," *New York Times*, 29 September 2002; Henry A. Wallace Center, op. cit. note 45, p. 20, and Tim Payne, United States Department of Agriculture, e-mail to author, 16 April 2002; British markets from Policy Commission on the Future of Farming and Food, op. cit. note 15, p. 45, and <www.farm ersmarkets.net>.

47. Costa Rica from Katherine Diaz-Knauf et al., "A Comparison of Produce Prices in Costa Rica: Farmers' Markets, Produce Markets, and Supermarkets," *Journal of Consumer Studies and Home Economics*, March 1992, pp. 106-17; United Kingdom from Foundation for Local Food Initiatives, "Shopping Basket Survey for South West Local Food Partnership," (London: 2002), <www.southwest foodlinks.org.uk>; United States from Robert Sommer et al., "Price Savings to Consumers at Farmers' Markets," *Journal of Consumer Affairs*, Winter 1980, pp. 452-62; more recent unpublished studies from Sommer, discussion with author, 23 February 2002; and unpublished surveys (showing that farmers' market produce is generally 10 to 20 percent cheaper than supermarket produce) by Ramu Govindasamy, Department of Agricultural, Food, and Resource Economics, Rutgers University, New Brunswick, New Jersey, e-mail to author, 19 September 2002. Farmers' markets as opportunities for small farmers from Henry A. Wallace Center, op. cit. note 45, p. 21.

48. Structure of community supported agriculture arrangements from Elizabeth Henderson and Robyn Van En, *Sharing the Harvest: A Guide to Community-Supported Agriculture* (White River Junction, Vermont: Chelsea Green Publishing Company, June 1999); number of such schemes from Henry A. Wallace Center, op. cit. note 45, p. 17; United Kingdom from Soil Association, "How To Set Up a Vegetable Box Scheme," Briefing Paper, Bristol, U.K., <www.soil association.org>, 8 July 2002.

49. Henderson and Van En, op. cit. note 48, and Dan Imhoff, "Linking Tables to Farms," in Eric T. Freyfogle (ed.), *The New Agrarianism: Land, Culture, and the Community of Life* (Washington, D.C.: Island Press, 2001), pp. 19-26.

50. Andy Fisher, Community Food Security Coalition, discussion with author, 5 February 2002.

51. Problems with processing and retailing units for small, local initiatives from Henry A. Wallace Center, op. cit. note 45, p. 35, and Policy Commission on the Future of Farming and Food, op. cit. note 15, p. 45; annual sales for

Sysco from Sysco Corporation, *2001 Annual Report* (Houston, TX: 2001), p. 1.

52. Jim Cheatle and Jane Tum, Association for Better Land Husbandry, Nairobi, Kenya, discussion with author, 14 February 2001; Lucie Rogo, International Center for Insect Physiology and Ecology, Nairobi, Kenya, discussion with author, 18 February 2001.

53. Dolan et al., op. cit. note 25; Cheatle and Tum, op. cit. note 52.

54. Azam-Ali, op. cit. note 45, and International Technology Development Group website, "Agroprocessing," <www.itdg.org>, viewed 4 September 2002.

55. Michael Gezana, technology area manager, International Technology Development Group (ITDG), Harare, Zimbabwe, e-mail to author, 22 August 2002, and ITDG, op. cit. note 54; opportunities for women in agroprocessing from United Nations Food and Agriculture Organization, op. cit. note 38, p. 19.

56. Azam-Ali, op. cit. note 45; United Nations Food and Agriculture Organization, op. cit. note 38, p. 18.

57. Azam-Ali, op. cit. note 45; barriers in the retailing sector and statistics on where most people buy food from Policy Commission on the Future of Farming and Food, op. cit. note 15, pp. 16, 45.

58. Institute for Agriculture and Trade Policy, *Marketing Sustainable Agriculture: Case Studies and Analysis From Europe* (Minneapolis, Minnesota: 1999), pp. 9, 16.

59. Mary Hendrickson, University of Missouri (Columbia), discussion with author, 4 March 2002.

60. Saritha Rai, "Battling to Satisfy India's Taste for Ice Cream, Farmers' Co-op Pesters Unilever," *New York Times*, 20 August 2002, and Amul website, <www.amul.com/gcmmf.html>, viewed 20 September 2002.

61. Institute for Agriculture and Trade Policy, op. cit. note 58, p. 11.

62. Food shops in the U.K. from ibid., p. 16; Christies Farm Shop from James Petts, "Public Procurement of Sustainable Food: Current, Planned, and Related Initiatives," Sustainable Food Chains Briefing Paper 3 (draft), published by Sustain, London, sent to author 1 August 2002.

63. Institute for Agriculture and Trade Policy, op. cit. note 58, p. 17.

64. Pamela J. King, "A Sea of Greens," *Rural Cooperatives*, U.S. Department of Agriculture, July/August 1999.

65. Petts, op. cit. note 62.

66. Sustain: The Alliance for Better Food and Farming, "Study Visit to Italy: The Italian School Meals System," <www.sustainweb.org/chain_italy_study.asp>, viewed 1 September 2002, and Petts, op. cit. note 62.

67. University of North Iowa Local Food Project, <www.uni.edu/ceee/food project/>, viewed 31 July 2002.

68. W.K. Kellogg Foundation, "Food for Thought: Community-Based Food Systems Enterprises" (report), Battle Creek, Michigan, 2002, p. 7, and Leslie Schaller, "Many Cooks Make a Restaurant Success," *In Business*, March/April 2000, pp. 12-15.

69. Jules Pretty, *The Living Land* (London: Earthscan, 1998), pp. 164, 165.

70. Puget Consumers' Cooperative from PCC Natural Markets website, <www.pccnaturalmarkets.com>, viewed 24 July 2002; Trudy Bialic, public affairs manager for PCC Natural Markets, discussion with author, 4 September 2002; and Adrienne P. Touart, "The Nation's Largest Natural Food Co-op," *In Business*, November/December 1999, pp. 23, 24.

71. Rhian Evans, community development worker, Hartcliffe Health & Environment Action Group, discussion with author, 12 August 2002; and Hartcliffe Health & Environment Action Group, *Annual Report: April 2000-March 2001*, Bristol, U.K., 2001.

72. Leopold Center for Sustainable Agriculture, "Our Rural Supermarket: Locally Grown Foods," *Center Progress Report*, May 2002, pp. 60, 61; Policy Commission on the Future of Farming and Food, op. cit. note 15, p. 45; Institute for Agriculture and Trade Policy, op. cit. note 58, p. 48.

73. Lindsay Howerton, "Patchwork Family Farms Finds New Markets," *In Motion Magazine*, 20 June 1999.

74. Institute for Agriculture and Trade Policy, op. cit. note 58, pp. 43-44; Neil Hamilton, "Putting a Face on Our Food: How State and Local Food Policies Can Promote the New Agriculture," *Drake Journal of Agricultural Law*, Volume 7, Issue 2, November 2002 (forthcoming), and "Attracting Consumers With Locally Grown Products," prepared for the North Central Initiative for Small Farm Profitability by the Food Processing Center, Institute of Agriculture and Natural Resources, University of Nebraska, Lincoln, October 2001, pp. 66, 67; Day Chocolate Company from Kika Dixon, The Day Chocolate Company, e-mail to Arunima Dhar (Worldwatch Institute), 1 August 2002, and <www.divine chocolate.com>, viewed 1 August 2002.

75. Organic Valley, *2001 CROPP Annual Report* (La Farge, Wisconsin: 2002), pp. 2, 3; and "Organic Valley Celebrates Nation's First Ever National Program of Regional Organic Milks," Organic Valley press release, La Farge, Wisconsin, <www.organicvalley.com>, 7 March 2002.

76. Jack Kloppenburg, Department of Rural Sociology, University of Wisconsin (Madison), discussion with author, 23 April 2002.

77. Estimate of the number of food policy councils from Hamilton, op. cit. note 74; estimate for councils outside of North America from Kameshwari Pothukuchi, Wayne State University, discussion with author, 3 March 2002; characteristics of the councils from Pothukuchi and Kaufman, op. cit. note 17, and Hamilton, op. cit. note 74. Box 4 from the following sources: Mark Winne, executive director, Hartford Food System, discussion with author, 4 April 2002, and Hartford Food System, <www.hartfordfood.org>, viewed 1 September 2002; Ian Hutchcroft, Devon Foodlinks, discussion with author, 21 April 2002, and Charles Couzens, Emma Delow and Sarah Watson, "Local Food Links in the South West of England, Summary Report," The Foundation for Local Food Initiatives, Bristol, United Kingdom, March 2001; Herb Barbolet, Farm Folk/City Folk, discussion with author, 20 May 2002, and <www.ffcf.bc.ca>, viewed 1 September 2002; Roberts, op. cit. note 39; and Toronto Food Policy Council, <www.city.toronto.on.ca/health/tfpc_index.htm>, viewed 23 August 2002.

78. Winne, op. cit. note 77.

79. Edward Seidler, United Nations Food and Agricultural Organization Marketing Group, e-mail to author, 11 July 2002; United Nations Food and Agricultural Organization, op. cit. note 38, pp. 45, 6; Frances Moore Lappé and Anna Lappé, *Hope's Edge: The Next Diet for a Small Planet* (New York: Tarcher/ Putnam, 2002), pp. 93-101.

80. Hutchcroft, op. cit. note 77; and Couzens, Delow, and Watson, op. cit. note 77.

81. Leslie Schaller, ACENet, e-mail to author, 26 July 2002; Mary McVay and Madi Hirschland, "Making the Connection: Appalachian Center for Economic Networks (ACENet)," Access to Markets Case Study Series, No. 1, The Aspen Institute, Washington, D.C., September 2000; Wayne Roberts, "The Way to a City's Heart Is Through Its Stomach: Putting Food Security on the Urban Planning Menu," Crackerbarrel Philosophy Series, Toronto Food Policy Council, Toronto, Ontario, June 2001, pp. 55-58.

82. Local procurement from Neil Hamilton, Agricultural Law Center, Drake University, discussion with author, 3 March 2002; Eaton and Abbeystead from Pretty, op. cit. note 69, p. 200.

83. Wegmans from Tom Furphy, former controller, Wegmans Food Markets, "Wegmans, Delivering Value to the Customer," presentation given at "The Food System of the 21st Century: Strategic Opportunities and Challenges," Kellogg Center, Michigan State University, East Lansing, Michigan, 7-9 February 2000; Policy Commission on the Future of Farming and Food, op. cit. note 15, pp. 45, 46.

84. Procurement restrictions in trade agreements from David Ferguson and James Petts of Sustain: The Alliance for Better Food and Farming, London, U.K., e-mail to author, 1 August 2002; see also Article III in the World Trade Organization Agreement on Government Procurement, <www.wto.org/english/tratop_e/gproc_e/agrmnt_e.htm>, and Articles 3 and 12 in Treaty Establishing the European Community, <www.europa.eu.int/eur-lex/en/treaties/dat/ec_cons_treaty_en.pdf>; "Japan Defends Its Protection of Farming Sector," *Associated Press*, 9 May 2002; Rosset, op. cit. note 34 (discussion). Box 6 from the following sources: $320 billion from Organisation for Economic Cooperation and Development (OECD), *Agricultural Policies in OECD Countries: Monitoring and Evaluation 2001* (Paris: 2001), pp. 25, 178, 183, 184; Rich Pirog, Leopold Center for Sustainable Agriculture, Iowa State University, Ames, Iowa, discussion with author, 28 August 2002.

85. Nabhan, op. cit. note 9; Gussow, op. cit. note 14, pp. 82, 83.

86. Comparison with 1967 foot-and-mouth epidemic from Tim Lang, "Out of the Crisis, Let There Be Hope," *Daily Express*, 28 Feb 2001; feed from China from T.R. Reid, "Asian Meat Suspected as Source of Disease," *Washington Post*, 28 March 2001.

87. Marsha Bushwood, Consumer Research Division, Promar International, Cheshire, United Kingdom, discussion with author, 13 March 2002.

88. Ibid.; Policy Commission on the Future of Farming and Food, op. cit. note 15, p. 44.

89. Terrorist incidents and concern about food system tampering from Rebecca Gardyn, "What's Cooking," *American Demographics*, March 2002, p. 35. This food supply estimate comes from The Rodale Institute, *Empty Breadbasket: The Coming Challenge to America's Food Supply and What We Can Do About It* (Kutztown, Pennsylvania: Rodale Press, 1981), pp. 12-14. Medard Gable, an expert on food and energy who was an author of *Empty Breadbaskets* and now works with Global Links Consultants, suggested that given trends in the food industry in the last two decades, including the move away from keeping large inventories and toward just-in-time delivery, any storage or emergency stocks have likely dropped further. Medard Gable, Global Links Consultants, <www.globallinksconsultants.com>, discussion with author, 3 September 2002.

90. Carlo Petrini, president, Slow Food Movement, e-mail to author, 17 July 2002; tomatoes estimate from Sommer, op. cit. note 6. For an analysis of crop breeding and agricultural research priorities see Jim Hightower, *Hard Tomatoes, Hard Times* (Cambridge, Massachusetts: Schenkman Publishing Co., 1978).

91. Slow Food membership and philosophy from Ilaria Morra, press office, Slow Food, e-mail to author, 14 July 2002, and Petrini, op. cit. note 90; Margaret Mead, "The Changing Significance of Food," *American Scientist*, March-April, 1970, pp. 176-81.

92. Justin Gillis, "Biotech Firms Launch Food Ad Blitz," *Washington Post*, 4 April 2000, and David Barboza, "Biotech Companies Take On Critics of Gene-Altered Food," *New York Times*, 12 November 1999.

93. JoAnn Jaffe and Michael Gertler, "Victual Vicissitudes: Consumer Deskilling and the Transformation of Food Systems," in M.D. Mehta (ed.), *The Sociology of Biotechnology* (Toronto: University Press, forthcoming).

94. Imhoff, op. cit. note 49, p. 20.

95. Jaffe and Gertler, op. cit. note 93.

96. Southwest England from Foundation for Local Food Initiatives, op cit. note 47; Hadley, Massachusetts from Imhoff, op. cit. note 49, p. 25; Fadzavanhu Enterprises from Gezana, op. cit. note 55.

Index

Other Worldwatch Papers

Other Publications From the Worldwatch Institute

State of the World 2003   Available January 2003
Worldwatch's flagship annual is used by government officials, corporate planners, journalists, development specialists, professors, students, and concerned citizens in over 120 countries. Published in more than 20 different languages, it is one of the most widely used resources for analysis.

State of the World Library 2003
Subscribe to the *State of the World Library* and join thousands of decisionmakers and concerned citizens who stay current on emerging environmental issues. The *State of the World Library* includes Worldwatch's flagship annuals, *State of the World* and *Vital Signs*, plus all four of the highly readable, up-to-date, and authoritative *Worldwatch Papers* as they are published throughout the calendar year.

Signposts 2002
This CD-ROM provides instant, searchable access to over 965 pages of full text from the last two editions of *State of the World* and *Vital Signs*, comprehensive data sets going back as far as 50 years, and easy-to-understand graphs and tables. Fully indexed, *Signposts 2002* contains a powerful search engine for effortless search and retrieval. Plus, it is platform independent and fully compatible with all Windows (3.1 and up), Macintosh, and Unix/Linux operating systems.

Vital Signs 2002
Written by Worldwatch's team of researchers, this annual provides comprehensive, user-friendly information on key trends and includes tables and graphs that help readers assess the developments that are changing their lives for better or for worse.

World Watch
This award-winning bimonthly magazine is internationally recognized for the clarity and comprehensiveness of its articles on global trends. Keep up to speed on the latest developments in population growth, climate change, species extinction, and the rise of new forms of human behavior and governance.

To make a tax-deductible contribution or to order any of Worldwatch's publications, call us toll-free at 888-544-2303 (or 570-320-2076 outside the U.S.), fax us at 570-322-2063, e-mail us at wwpub@worldwatch.org or visit our website at www.worldwatch.org.